Cosmic Engineers

COSMIC ENGINEERS

A Study of Hard Science Fiction

Gary Westfahl

Contributions to the Study of Science Fiction
and Fantasy, Number 67
Donald Palumbo, Series Adviser

GREENWOOD PRESS
Westport, Connecticut • London

Library of Congress Cataloging-in-Publication Data

Westfahl, Gary.
   Cosmic engineers : a study of hard science fiction / Gary
Westfahl.
     p. cm.—(Contributions to the study of science fiction and
fantasy ; ISSN 0193–6875, no. 67)
   Includes bibliographical references and index.
   ISBN 0–313–29727–4 (alk. paper)
   1. Science fiction, American—History and criticism.
2. Literature and technology—United States—History—20th century.
3. Literature and science—United States—History—20th century.
4. Space sciences in literature. I. Title. II. Series.
PS374.S35W43 1996
813′.0876209—dc20   95–4667

British Library Cataloguing in Publication Data is available.

Library of Congress Catalog Card Number: 95–4667
ISBN: 0–313–29727–4
ISSN: 0193–6875

First published in 1996

Greenwood Press, 88 Post Road West, Westport, CT   06881
An imprint of Greenwood Publishing Group, Inc.

Printed in the United States of America

The paper used in this book complies with the
Permanent Paper Standard issued by the National
Information Standards Organization (Z39.48–1984).

10 9 8 7 6 5 4 3 2 1

To my late father,

Wesley B. Westfahl

Contents

Acknowledgements

I first wish to thank David N. Samuelson of California State University, Long Beach, who first inspired me to study this subject as guest editor of a special issue of *Science-Fiction Studies* on hard science fiction. Later, he and R. D. Mullen of that journal agreed to publish in that issue an early draft of material incorporated into this book as "'The Closely Reasoned Technological Story': The Critical History of Hard Science Fiction." Thanks are next due to Damon Knight, who accepted a short version of Chapter 6 as an article in the third issue of *Monad: Essays on Science Fiction*, there entitled "Good Physics, Lousy Engineering: Arthur C. Clarke's *A Fall of Moondust*." I should also thank Gregory Benford, who helpfully read and responded to an early manuscript; Donald M. Hassler, who read and commented on a draft of Chapter 7; and Arthur B. Evans, who provided useful information on Jules Verne. Also deserving thanks are George Slusser and Eric S. Rabkin, whose anthology *Hard Science Fiction* was stimulating, though I came to disagree with many of its contributors. I thank Donald A. Palumbo for recommending this book to Greenwood Press, and Nina Pearlstein, Catherine A. Lyons, and others at that company who assisted in having the book approved and prepared for publication. Other colleagues in the field of science fiction criticism who have provided encouragement and support in a more general way include Stephen P. Brown, John Clute, Sheila Finch, Howard V. Hendrix, Edward James, Michael Burgess, David Pringle, and Milton T. Wolf.

In a different way, I should express my appreciation to the late Clifford D. Simak, who provided a most appropriate title for this study, even though the novel I borrowed my title from—his underrated space epic—was not otherwise relevant to the topic of hard science fiction. In a broader sense, I must thank all of the various writers and commentators whose observations permeate this book—principally the late P. Schuyler Miller; while the conclusions expressed here are entirely my own, their many remarks were very important to me in reaching these conclusions. In part, they are the true authors of this book, and I am merely compiling and interpreting their collective judgments.

Finally, as always, I thank my wife Lynne and children Allison and Jeremy for enduring my obsession with science fiction research; David Werner of the University of LaVerne's Educational Programs in Corrections for the occasional opportunity to teach science fiction classes; and Patrick J. Moran and my other colleagues at the Learning Center of the University of California at Riverside for their ongoing friendship and support.

Cosmic Engineers

1

Introduction

In many ways, the ongoing debate over the nature of hard science fiction mirrors the larger debate concerning the nature of science fiction itself. That is, there are many who seem to feel that the field is easily and exactly defined and many who find it extremely difficult to articulate such a definition. There are those who wish to expand the term to incorporate many texts that are not traditionally regarded as part of the field and those who wish to restrict the term to texts that are universally accepted as part of the field. Some argue that it is a relatively old form of writing, while some argue that it is a relatively new form of writing. Many want to maintain that its works constitute a unique and special type of fiction, and many want to maintain that its works are, on examination, actually similar to other comparable works of fiction.

While a study of hard science fiction thus might serve as a useful microcosm for a study of the entire genre, there are other reasons why this subgenre demands special consideration (though I might maintain polemically that a science fiction scholar requires no particular justification to closely examine any works of science fiction). Its practitioners and supporters often wish to argue that hard science fiction constitutes the "core" of science fiction, its purest and most special form, while other commentators sometimes wish to see hard science fiction as one of two broad movements in the genre, the other being "soft science fiction," which are forever locked in mortal combat to attain a position of centrality in science fiction. It is possible to question the validity of such arguments, and I will later be doing exactly that; nevertheless, such sweeping claims for the scope and importance of hard science fiction should be thoroughly investigated and evaluated before they are dismissed.

There have been, of course, other examinations of the field of hard science fiction, notably including George Slusser and Eric S. Rabkin's critical anthology *Hard Science Fiction* (1986), a special issue of *Science-Fiction Studies* to which

I contributed (July 1993), and numerous discussions in *The New York Review of Science Fiction* which culminated in David G. Hartwell and Kathryn Cramer's *The Ascent of Wonder: The Evolution of Hard Science Fiction* (1994), an anthology with extensive introductory commentaries. While much valuable work has been done, many contributions remain little more than expressions of personal opinion: One critic chooses a definition and texts that will best support her conclusions, then unsurprisingly employs that definition and those texts to reach those conclusions, while others choose different definitions and different texts to justify their different conclusions. And no critics have strong grounds for claiming that their opinions are superior to others' opinions.

As one important way to provide a more solid foundation for these studies, I have extensively researched the origins of the *idea* of hard science fiction and virtually all early uses of the term (Chapters 2 and 3). Etymology is not necessarily destiny, but the researchers for *The Oxford English Dictionary* who compile sentences illustrating all meanings of a word do so in part because knowing how a word has been used in the past is an important element in understanding its present range of meanings and uses. In the case of *hard science fiction*, virtually no work of this kind has been done; until I first reported my own research in 1993, for example, no one realized that the term was first used by P. Schuyler Miller in 1957. My evidence suggests two conclusions: First, there have regularly been efforts to expand the meaning of *hard science fiction* to apply to authors and texts that are not commonly associated with the term; second, there is a stronger tradition of efforts to restrict the term to a rather narrow range of authors and texts.

Next, as another key source of information about the parameters and nature of hard science fiction, I have closely studied the comments and essays of several writers commonly associated with the subgenre (Chapter 4). Surely, though authors are not always reliable explicators of their own works, these people qualify as privileged commentators on the field, and their observations provide additional data about the characteristic purposes and forms of hard science fiction.

Deriving from these sources a preliminary sense of the nature of hard science fiction, I then seek to clarify the history of the subgenre (Chapter 5): At what time did texts first emerge that one might reasonably regard as hard science fiction?

With this work completed, it seemed appropriate to examine three representative works to gain a better understanding of the priorities that govern the writing of hard science fiction and of the fundamental limitations of the form (Chapters 6, 7, and 8). Focusing on a few novels is often necessary for critics in an imperfect world who have a finite amount of time to complete their research; still, since the texts a critic chooses may be criticized as inappropriate or self-serving, I should explain the rationale behind my decisions. Arthur C. Clarke's *A Fall of Moondust* was, to my knowledge, the first work identified as hard science fiction at the time of first publication; from a strictly nominalist viewpoint, it might be regarded as the first hard science fiction novel, and that is why I was first attracted to it. Because Hal Clement's *Mission of Gravity* is so often described as the quintessential work of hard science fiction, its inclusion seemed inescapable. Charles Sheffield's *Between the Strokes of Night* is admittedly a less obvious choice, and several other novels might have been selected to represent its type; here, my motive was in part to draw more critical attention to this interesting author and his work.

Finally, to draw all my conclusions together, I offer a preliminary description of the subgenre of hard science fiction and a few comments about its nature and possible future (Chapter 9). No doubt, there is an element of subjectivity in the ways I have interpreted my data; still, statements that are supported by several quotations from different sources are, I believe, more valuable, and harder to dismiss, than statements supported only by the reputations of their authors.

I should say a word about the extent of the research that underlies those conclusions. First, I examined a large number of books and magazines from the 1950s and earlier (including many that are not mentioned) and found a few terms that are arguably equivalent to hard science fiction, but I was generally persuaded that the term itself was not being used at the time. Moving on to the 1960s, my discovery that Miller employed the term in a 1963 book review for *Analog Science Fact/Science Fiction* inspired a thoroughgoing examination of all his reviews and review columns from 1944 to 1975; also from the 1960s, I read James Blish's review columns as collected in *The Issue at Hand* and *More Issues at Hand*, Algis Budrys's review columns as collected in *Benchmarks: Galaxy Bookshelf*, and Judith Merril's uncollected review columns for *The Magazine of Fantasy and Science Fiction*. I also examined a large number of other secondary texts from the 1960s and 1970s, searching for references to hard science fiction, conducted a cursory survey of recent critical literature, and made a special effort to examine all of the writings of major hard science fiction writers—including Clement, Clarke, Poul Anderson, Gregory Benford, Robert F. Forward, and Larry Niven—about their and others' works.

Also, having explained what this book will accomplish, I should frankly state what it does not attempt to accomplish. First, while my B.A. in mathematics and experience teaching math at the college level arguably provide minimal qualifications, I am not a scientist and do not feel fully qualified to discuss purely scientific issues. My considerations of the complex relationship between science and hard science fiction will be limited to some basic comments about the scientific process and the eventual conclusion that some type of purely scientific evaluation is a necessary element in examinations of hard science fiction. Second, as David N. Samuelson's bibliography in the July 1993 issue of *Science-Fiction Studies* indicates, I have not read all critical works relevant to hard science fiction, primarily focusing instead on the comments and observations of nonacademic commentators—which have been, I believe, more

influential. Third, I do not offer anything resembling a comprehensive survey of
the literature of hard science fiction. The value of this book is that it represents
a useful starting point for studies of hard science fiction: Establishing its basic
parameters, clearing away some of the exaggerated claims and dubious criticisms
that have cluttered critical discussions, and identifying the fundamental issues
that scholars of this subgenre will need to confront.

   In short, there is one other way in which a study of hard science fiction
resembles a study of science fiction: No single book can pretend to cover the
field completely. While I can properly claim that I am making an important
contribution to the study of hard science fiction, much work remains to be done,
and I hope—and believe—that this book will be helpful to the others who will
continue that work.

2

"Science Fiction vs. Science Faction": Early Efforts to Define Scientific Science Fiction

When did the world first realize that what we now call science fiction in fact existed as a separate category of literature? Looking at the United States during the crucial decade of the 1920s, one can make two observations. First, a number of critical voices had already displayed a dim and scattered awareness that there was something distinctive in stories about amazing inventions, the future, and space travel, as evidenced by a number of terms occasionally used to describe such works: two terms from the late nineteenth century—the British *scientific romance* and the American *invention stories*—still surfaced at times, while publishers and magazine editors had devised a number of alternate terms, including *off-trail stories, impossible stories, different stories, highly imaginative stories, weird-scientific stories, pseudo-scientific stories, scientific fiction,* and *scientific novels.*[1] Second, however, because there was no commonly accepted term for this type of story, popular awareness of science fiction necessarily remained dim and scattered; with no consensus about what to call this genre, discussions of its nature and characteristics were sporadic and disconnected.

The person who changed this situation forever was Hugo Gernsback, who tirelessly proselytized for this form of literature throughout the period, calling it first *scientific fiction,* then *scientifiction,* and finally *science fiction.* A few years after it was officially introduced in June 1929, this latter term was universally adopted; and since Gernsback played such a key role in establishing public awareness of the genre, his ideas about science fiction dominated all commentaries on the subject and have remained influential to this day.

My first task here is to establish when the world first realized that a distinct subgenre of hard science fiction existed, and the crucial decade in examining this question is the 1950s. That is, by this time there had already been a number of efforts to name and describe a form of science fiction with unusual attentiveness to scientific accuracy and logic, while a lack of agreement on what to call such stories prevented the emergence of a true awareness of the form. It is possible, though, that the idea of hard science fiction could have appeared much earlier; for in a way, the concept is a natural response to a contradiction in Hugo Gernsback's public statements about science fiction that was immediately apparent.

On the first page of the first issue of his "scientifiction" magazine *Amazing Stories*, he editorially defined the genre as "a charming romance intermingled with scientific fact and prophetic vision," claiming that such works were "instructive. They supply knowledge that we might now otherwise obtain" ("A New Sort of Magazine" 3). Yet on the next page, introducing Jules Verne's *Off on a Comet*, he was obliged to offer a different message:

[T]he author here abandons his usual scrupulously scientific attitude and gives his fancy freer rein .... Verne asks us to accept a situation which is in a sense self-contradictory. The earth and a comet are brought twice into collision without mankind in general, or even our astronomers, becoming conscious of the fact. Moreover several people from widely scattered places are carried off by the comet and returned uninjured. Yet further, the comet snatches and carries away with it for the convenience of its travelers, both air and water. Little, useful tracts of earth are picked up and, as it were, turned over and clapped down right side up again upon the comet's surface. Even ships pass uninjured through this remarkable somersault. These events all belong to the realm of fairy-land. ("Introduction to This Story" 4-5)

Though Gernsback then praised these lapses as a vehicle for correct science elsewhere in the story, the situation remains paradoxical: After promising a magazine with stories containing accurate and educational scientific information, Gernsback's first task as its editor is to explain some blatant scientific inaccuracies in one of his stories. And in later issues of *Amazing Stories*, Gernsback published other stories whose scientific weaknesses could not be concealed by strained editorial explanations.[2] Discerning readers could reach only one conclusion: All science fiction stories were scientific, but some were more scientific than others.

In one editorial in the early 1930s, Gernsback publicly acknowledged that there were different degrees of attentiveness to science in the genre and proposed new terminology to describe two forms of science fiction:

In time to come, also, our authors will make a marked distinction between science fiction and science *faction*, if I may coin such a term .... In science fiction the author may fairly let his imagination run wild and, as long as he does not turn the story into an obvious fairy tale, he will still remain within the bounds of pure science fiction. Science fiction may be prophetic fiction, in that the things imagined by the author may come true some time; even if this "some time" may mean a hundred thousand years hence .... In sharp counter-distinction to science fiction, we also have science *faction*. By this term I mean science fiction in which there are so many scientific facts that the story, as far as the scientific part is concerned, is no longer fiction but becomes more or less a recounting of fact.

For instance, if one spoke of rocket-propelled fliers a few years ago, such machines obviously would have come under the heading of science fiction. Today such fliers properly come under the term science *faction*; because the rocket is a fact today .... the few experimenters who have worked with rocket-propelled machines have had sufficient encouragement to enable us to predict quite safely that during the next twenty-five years, rocket flying will become the order of the day ("Science Fiction vs. Science Faction" 5).

While not a complete description of the types of stories that would later be regarded as belonging to the subgenre, Gernsback's editorial can still be read as the first manifesto on behalf of hard science fiction: He is attempting to isolate, define, and defend a special type of science fiction where scientific accuracy is most central. He even goes so far as to describe the particular audience for this new subgenre: "[T]he man of science, the research worker, and even the hard-headed business man will perhaps look with more favor upon science *faction* because here he will get valuable information that may be of immediate use; whereas the information contained in the usual run of science fiction may perhaps be too far in advance of the times and may often be thought to be too fantastic to be of immediate use to humanity" (5). There is even a hint that Gernsback prefers this type of science fiction in his rather dismissive contrasting reference to "the usual run of science fiction."

Had Gernsback devoted more time to presenting and explaining this term, or had readers responded enthusiastically to it, a concept similar to hard science fiction might have emerged in the 1930s. However, this was the only time Gernsback ever used this term, and there was no visible reader response. Instead, after years of defending dubiously scientific stories, and after once introducing terminology that might have sanctioned such works as a form of science fiction, Gernsback soon launched an extraordinary attack on the fanciful science in a story he was publishing—John W. Campbell, Jr.'s "Space Rays":

When science fiction first came into being, it was taken most seriously by all authors. In practically all instances, authors laid the basis of their stories upon a solid scientific foundation. If an author made a statement as to certain future instrumentalities, he usually found it advisable to adhere closely to the possibilities of science as it was then known.

Many modern science fiction authors have no such scruples. They do not hesitate to throw scientific plausibility overboard, and embark on a policy of what I might call scientific magic, in other words, science that is neither plausible, nor possible. Indeed, it overlaps the fairy tale, and often goes the fairy tale one better .... In the present offering, Mr. John W. Campbell, Jr., has no doubt realized this state of affairs and has proceeded in an earnest way to burlesque some of our rash authors to whom plausibility and possible science mean nothing. He pulls, magician-like, all sorts of impossible rays from his silk hat, much as a magician extracts rabbits .... I have gone to this length to preach a sermon in the hope that misguided authors will see the light, and hereafter stick to science as it is known, or as it may reasonably develop in the future ("Reasonableness in Science Fiction" 585).

Here, Gernsback forcefully reintroduced his first claim: all true science fiction was built on a "solid scientific foundation"; a story without a scientific basis was a "fairy tale." And this remained the party line of commentators throughout the 1930s and 1940s: While published stories displayed wide variations in their concern for science, all editors—even those of magazines whose disregard for scientific rigor was blatant—continued to publicly insist that their stories were scientifically defensible.

Nevertheless, in the 1940s, there were a few efforts to name a special form of science fiction focused on science. In 1948, for example, John W. Campbell, Jr., listed the *gadget story* as one of the "three broad types" of science fiction ("Introduction," *Who Goes There?* 3), and the term appeared occasionally in the 1940s and 1950s, as in Basil Davenport's 1955 *Inquiry into Science Fiction* (31) and Robert A. Heinlein's 1959 essay "Science Fiction: Its Nature, Faults, and Virtues" (16). However, the idea of stories about machines hardly qualifies as a fair description of hard science fiction, and people like Campbell generally used the term as a criticism, a way to label outdated and inferior stories which lacked the deeper social awareness and improved writing of modern authors. Given these connotations, people could not have employed the term as the basis for a *defense* of scientific science fiction; and for that reason, perhaps, the term was never popular.

Another term that cropped up in discussions among science fiction fans was the *scientific problem story*, referring to stories—associated with writers like Ross Rocklynne, George O. Smith, and Jack Williamson writing as "Will Stewart"—that as the name implied focused on a scientific puzzle which heroes, and readers, are challenged to solve. But this term rarely if ever entered prominently published commentaries—although Davenport's "chess-problem type of story" in reference to Hal Clement's *Mission of Gravity* came close (33)—and, like *gadget story*, was far too limited in its implications to serve as a description of a literature of hard science fiction.

Undoubtedly, there were other, little-noted attempts to establish a special category of science-oriented science fiction. For example, Paul Carter's "You Can Write Science Fiction If You Want To" cites a letter from the November 1950 issue of *Planet Stories* that suggests a division of the field similar to Gernsback's: "[T]here are types of stf [scientifiction]: there's the 'scientific' science fiction as represented by ASF [*Astounding Science-Fiction*], and there's the so-called 'thud-and-blunder' science fiction as represented by *Planet*. I don't see how anyone can say that one is any better than the other .... *[B]oth* are science fiction" (cited by Carter 150).

In the period following World War II, the number of references to science fiction stories emphasizing science dramatically increased. In 1947, Robert A. Heinlein, after discussing stories with some characteristics later associated with hard science fiction, finally came up with the phrase "the Simon-pure science fiction story" ("On the Writing of Speculative Fiction" 18). In 1949, Melvin Korshak introduced the term "heavy science story" to describe one type of science fiction ("Introduction: Trends in Modern Science-Fiction" 18). In a talk for the Cambridge University English Club in 1955, C. S. Lewis, listing what he termed "subgenres" of science fiction, discussed "Engineers' Stories,"

written by people who are primarily interested in space-travel, or in other undiscovered techniques, as real possibilities. They give us in imaginative form their guesses as to how the thing might be done. Jules Verne's *Twenty Thousand Leagues Under the Sea* and Wells's *Land Ironclads* were once specimens of this kind .... Arthur C. Clarke's *Prelude to Space* is another. I am too uneducated scientifically to criticize such stories on the mechanical side; and I am so completely out of sympathy with the projects they anticipate that I am incapable of criticizing them as stories. ("On Science Fiction" 62-63)

In a telephone conversation, Gregory Benford recalled a talk with Poul Anderson in the early 1960s when they used the phrase "Campbellian science fiction," while Harlan Ellison employed the similar "Campbellesque science fiction," as well as "the Campbell heavy-science story" and "the Campbell dull-science novel," to describe Frank Herbert's *The Dragon in the Sea* in 1968 ("A Voice from the Styx" 122, 123, 125). In their 1966 introduction to Clarke's "The Wind from the Sun" (then called "Sunjammer"),[3] Donald A. Wollheim and Terry Carr observed, "Just as the mystery field has a sub-genre called 'police procedural fiction' ... a type of story so integrally concerned with how the future will work ... might be called 'procedural science fiction'—and Arthur C. Clarke, with tales like PRELUDE TO SPACE and A FALL OF MOONDUST, has shown that he is the master of the form" (*World's Best Science Fiction: 1966* 9). And during the mid-1960s, Judith Merril employed what could be seen as a synonym for hard science fiction—"solid science fiction" ("Books," *The Magazine of Fantasy and Science Fiction*, August 1966 63; January 1967 63).

Just as one can detect various aspects of the idea of science fiction in terms like *scientific romance*, *invention story*, *impossible story*, and *pseudo-scientific story*, one can see a nascent concept of hard science fiction in terms like *gadget story*, *scientific problem story*, *Engineers' Story*, and *solid science fiction*. However, in order for the subgenre to become truly established, there would have to be someone like Hugo Gernsback to create and popularize one standard term and define the characteristics of the form. As it happens, that person was P. Schuyler Miller, science fiction writer and, for twenty-four years, regular book reviewer for *Astounding Science-Fiction* and its successors *Analog: Science*

Fact/Science Fiction and *Analog: Science Fiction/Science Fact.*

Some may be surprised to hear P. Schuyler Miller mentioned as an important figure in science fiction history, because in discussions of major book reviewers of the 1950s and 1960s, only two names come up regularly—Damon Knight and James Blish. And with good reason: Both men were also well-known as superior science fiction writers, and both wrote about science fiction with unusual eloquence and keen insight. In contrast, Miller never established himself as a significant author, and he was never renowned either for his prose or for his critical acumen; Malcolm J. Edwards notes, for instance, that he "was not a particularly demanding critic" ("P. Schuyler Miller" 808). Still, while he was clearly not the best reviewer of his day, one can argue that he was the most influential reviewer—for two reasons.

The first reason is, in a sense, the story of the Tortoise and the Hare. Knight and Blish concentrated on reviewing for less than a decade, and their writings appeared sporadically in a variety of places, often little-known publications. While later collections of their reviews (Knight's *In Search of Wonder* and Blish's *The Issue at Hand* and *More Issues at Hand*) added to their visibility, their failure to become regular and prominently published reviewers undoubtedly diminished their impact. In contrast, Miller presented reviews in what was consistently the best-selling science fiction magazine every month (with occasional missing months) for twenty-four years, from 1951 until 1975. In sum, writers and readers may have admired Knight and Blish more, but they surely read Miller more, and more often.

Second, Miller's notably different priorities in writing reviews contributed to his influence. As clearly announced in the opening manifestos of their collections, Knight and Blish saw their purpose as nothing else than the improvement of all science fiction. In reviewing good books, they would emphasize the features that made them good, and in reviewing bad books, they would identify the features that made them bad. By doing so, they could train writers to produce better science fiction, and they could encourage readers to seek out and read better science fiction. In this way, science fiction would get better and better, as inferior writers were gradually eliminated, either by reeducation or by impoverishment.

Miller's goals were more modest. With no concern for addressing writers, he wrote for an imagined audience of readers who wanted to read science fiction and needed advice on what books they should read. In order to do this, he would need to summarize the plot of each book, explain what type of book it was, and offer some judgment about its overall quality. (The title that Campbell chose for Miller's column—"The Reference Library"—was thus unusually apt; Miller essentially envisioned himself as a helpful librarian, who might be approached by a patron who said, "I like to read colorful science fiction adventures with a touch of science—what do you recommend?")

It was in fulfilling this second purpose—classification—that Miller perhaps had his greatest effects. Despite efforts to blur science fiction and fantasy (as in the title of *The Magazine of Fantasy and Science Fiction*), Miller saw the two forms as distinct and tried to review only science fiction; in discussing a mixed anthology, he would literally list every story and classify it as either science fiction or fantasy. Miller identified works as juvenile science fiction, which he saw as a potentially worthwhile form in itself. He freely adapted descriptive terms developed by others, such as *thud-and-blunder story*, *space opera*, and *sword-and-sorcery*, and surprisingly, in 1961, he may have become the first person to use the phrase *New Wave* in reference to emerging British writers.[4] With further research, Miller might be established as a key figure in establishing and popularizing many terms for subgenres of science fiction that are now in general use.

However, there was one particular form of science fiction that Miller needed to label and discuss for readers of *Astounding Science-Fiction*: stories with a heavy dose of science. This was, presumably, what readers of Campbell's magazine were largely interested in. For that reason, perhaps, Miller was unusually energetic in identifying and describing works of that type.

Some of the terms he employed seem primarily designed to distinguish science fiction from fantasy and do not have a great deal of relevance to his emerging efforts to characterize what we now call hard science fiction. One of these was *"straight"* science fiction. He said "Hal Clement excels at the kind of straight science fiction, a step beyond Heinlein's, in which he takes equal pains to work out an adventure as seen by, and directed by the peculiar nature of, an alien form of life" ("The Reference Library," November 1954 147);[5] and reviewing *The Best from Fantasy and Science Fiction: Tenth Series*, he called Richard McKenna's "Mine Own Ways" and Poul Anderson's "Martyr" the "only two stories in the lot that could be called 'straight' science fiction" (October 1961 166). Another was *"real"* science fiction. He spoke of Clement's *Mission of Gravity* and Clarke's *Prelude to Space* as "two top examples of heavy-science books ... *real* science fiction" (November 1956 156); he said that John W. Campbell, Jr.'s *Islands of Space*, Murray Leinster's *Colonial Survey* and Clement's *Cycle of Fire* "seem to me to be examples of what some readers mean when they say they want 'real' science fiction" (November 1957 142); *Lucky Starr and the Rings of Saturn* was "the kind of thing we expect of [Isaac] Asimov and of 'real' science fiction" (February 1959 140); noting Gordon R. Dickson's *Secret under the Sea*, he said, "More and more 'real' science fiction is also being written for the younger set" (January 1962 156); and he called Clarke's *The Deep Range* "what engineers call the 'real' science fiction, almost documentary in its technical perfection" (June 1962 159).[6] Four other terms were used rarely: *Main-line science fiction*—"by 'main-line,' I mean stories in which the backgrounds are meticulously worked out and the story grows out of them" (May 1954 149); *"pure" science fiction*—"where 'pure' science fiction ... would have developed this picture through action, [Bernard Wolfe's] 'Limbo' does it through talk and more talk" (January 1954 149); *out-and-out science fiction*—"only half a dozen [stories in an anthology] are out-and-out science fiction" (December 1953 145); and the *science-based SF story*—Campbell's *Islands of Space*, Murray Leinster's *Colonial Survey* and Clement's *Cycle of Fire* show "an increasing degree of sophistication in the science-based SF story" (November 1957 145).

One very early and very specialized term related to scientific science fiction was the *super-physics type of story*, used to described E. E. Smith's *Skylark Three* ("Book Reviews," September 1949 152); before, he had said that Smith's Skylark books "introduce[d] the 'super-physics' field of science fiction" ("Book Reviews," October 1947 104); and he later called John W. Campbell, Jr.'s *The Mightiest Machine* "perhaps the climax of the super-physics school of science fiction" ("Book Reviews," November 1950 94).

"Documentary" science fiction, as in the preceding statement about Clarke's *The Deep Range*, was another relevant experiment. He said Clarke's *Prelude to Space* "has all the 'documentary' quality of [the film] 'Destination Moon'" (November 1954 151); he called Clarke's *The City and the Stars* "the poetic—as distinguished from the documentary—Clarke" (July 1956 155); later that year, he spoke of the "three major divisions of science fiction: the literary fantasy, the sociological, and the documentary" (November 1956 154-155); in May 1957, he noted "the documentary realism of Clarke" (147); *The Deep Range* "fits with 'Prelude to Space' and 'Sands of Mars' among the 'documentaries' that Arthur Clarke has made all his own" (September 1957 145); Rex Gordon's *First on Mars* was "an ideal example of the underplayed 'documentary'" (February 1958 146); *The Deep Range* was "Another of Clarke's documentaries-with-action" (July 1959 158); noticing a poll that listed *Childhood's End* as a favorite novel, he said "The poetic, rather than the documentary Clarke is the one you remember most fondly" (October 1959 143); Jeff Sutton's *Spacehive* "has the same kind of documentary competence that we expect of someone like Arthur C. Clarke" (July 1961 158); Clarke's *Prelude to Space* was "one of his best documentaries" (April 1962 167) and his "classic 'documentary' of man's first adventure into space" (April 1970 170); and, speaking of Lewis, Miller said that his term *Engineers' story* is "what I call the documentary approach of Arthur Clarke and much of Verne" (August 1967 166).

A few times, he simply italicized the word *science* to establish a special category: Raymond Jones's "Production Test" "is that rare yarn, a *science* fiction story" (July 1954 150); he spoke of Clement's "solid *science* fiction" (October 1954 148), and said that "the ultimate in present-day *science* fiction is being written by Hal Clement" (November 1957 145); George O. Smith writes "the kind of oldish-fashioned *science* fiction yarn he can do so well" (February 1959 142); and Clement's *Mission of Gravity* is "one of the classics of recent *science fiction*" (February 1959 149).

At least two of these variant terms employed the word *hard*. One of these was *"hard science"* story. In August 1959, he said James Blish's *The Triumph of Time* "is almost an anachronism: a 'hard science' story in the vein of E. E. Smith's 'Skylark' yarns, of John W. Campbell's 'Mightiest Machine' series of nearly twenty years ago .... [O]ne reader I know considered the discussion of the scientific problem so much technical double-talk" (151). In September 1961, he called Blish's *Titan's Daughter* "a 'hard science' story" (167), and in January 1963, he said that Clarke's "A Slight Case of Sunstroke" "is gorgeous corn and 'hard' science at the same time" (172).

Miller continued to occasionally employ this term well after he had regularly taken to speaking of hard science fiction. In May 1964, he said Fred and Geoffrey Hoyle's *Fifth Planet* was "to a degree a 'hard'-type story which might even stir some interest in Hal Clement, chief sculptor of that form among us" (87); he cited Arthur C. Clarke's "Maelstrom II" as "one of the 'hard science' stories [in Judith Merril's *11th Annual Edition: The Year's Best S-F*] and in the author's best documentary mode" (June 1967 164); he called Larry Niven's "Neutron Star" "an excellent 'hard science' yarn" (March 1968 162) and "a 'hard science' short story" (August 1971 166); he said that Niven "combines 'hard' science and swashbuckling action in a way that nobody else has done in years, if ever" (August, 1971 165); he commented that "[t]hough [Poul Anderson] isn't one of the writer you ordinarily think of as a 'hard science' man, he can write some very hard science into some very lively plots" (April 1970 168); he said that a runaway ship nearing the speed of light "is the 'hard science' framework" of Anderson's *Tau Zero* (January 1971 167); he observed that "[s]ome, or most, *writers* can't mix 'hard' science with the structure of a detective story" (June 1971 169); he said Ben Bova's "Zero Gee" was one of *Again, Dangerous Visions*'s "few, and good 'hard' science stories, a near documentary" and Frederik Pohl's "The Merchants of Venus" (later incorporated into *The Gateway Trip*) was "the hardest 'hard science' story the author has written" (April 1973 170, 171); Poul Anderson's "Lodestar" "utilizes a new hard science concept" and Clement's "Lecture Demonstration" is "a hard-science problem story set on Mesklin" (March 1974 168); Anderson's "In the Shadow" "is that self-contradictory thing, a 'hard science' story from Fantasy and Science Fiction" (June 1974 168); in one anthology, he said, there were "three stories that could be most properly called 'hard science'"—Larry Niven's "Rammer," James Blish's "Darkside Crossing," and Stephen Tall's "Allison, Carmichael, and Tattersall" (July 1974 160); and he said that Clarke's *Rendezvous with Rama* "is a 'hard science' book in the classic tradition" (September 1974 170).

Forms of the term *hard science story*—including use of *hard science* as an adjective without *fiction*—were sometimes used by other commentators in the 1960s and 1970s: in 1968, Harlan Ellison said that in writing *Dragonflight*, Anne McCaffrey "has taken as her tools the form and content of the most masculine specie of speculative fiction: the hard science adventure novel" ("A Voice from the Styx" 138), and in 1969, Anthony Lewis called McCaffrey's "A Meeting of Minds" "a hard-science sf love story" ("Magazine Reviews" [7]). In 1974, Gregory Benford said that Heinlein "is well known as a 'hard' science writer" ("Science and Science Fiction" 34). In 1976, Richard A. Lupoff spoke of "the 'hard science' stories of Jules Verne a century ago and of Hal Clement and Larry Niven today" (cited in Bainbridge 28). In that year, C. L. Grant noted that "magazines (like *Analog*) specialize in stories that are highly extrapolative, emphasizing the 'hard-science' aspects of SF" ("Introduction: Getting Your Feet Wet" 20), and George R. R. Martin identified Poul Anderson and Larry Niven as "prominent modern author[s] of the hard science school" ("First, Sew On a Tentacle" 163). Two years later, Poul Anderson said that "Verne embodied 'hard' science and technophilia" (cited in Bainbridge 29). To this day, the expression is often employed.

Some may wonder why I carefully isolate these references to *hard science stories* from my forthcoming description of references to *hard science fiction*, since they appear to be synonymous and, in fact, are sometimes used interchangeably—as in, for example, William Bainbridge's *Dimensions of Science Fiction*. However, there is an importance difference between the terms. In *hard science story* or variant expressions, *hard science* must be read as a phrasal noun modifying *story*, so the meaning of the term is "a story about or involving hard science." In *hard science fiction*, the phrasal noun is *science fiction*, modified by the adjective *hard*, so the meaning of the term is "science fiction that is in some way hard." Clearly, then, *hard science fiction* can be read and applied more broadly than *hard science story*; and, as I will discuss, the term *hard science fiction* has in the hands of some commentators actually expanded beyond any association with hard science.

A final, less common alternative term used by Miller was *hard-shell science fiction*. In one review, while elsewhere speaking of the "hard-shell purist" who could "itemize a good many places [in Alfred Bester's *The Stars My Destination*] in which the science *per se* won't hold water—or even molasses," Miller said that "where John Campbell's yarns were 'hard sell' [surely a misprint for *hard shell*], Leinster's are fashionably 'soft'" (November 1957 148, 145). Later, he described Philip K. Dick's *Time Out of Joint* as "good, hard-shell science fiction" (January 1960 174).[7]

Reading through all of Miller's review columns in the late 1950s and early 1960s, one can observe the reviewer shifting back and forth between various terms, sometimes employing one almost exclusively for a few months before reverting to older terms or developing a new one. For a while, it seemed that he would settle on *hard science story* as the standard term; however, he had by 1960 also come up with, and used a couple of times, a slightly different term, *hard science fiction*, and by the mid-1960s that would emerge as his clear favorite. And the entire science fiction community would follow his lead.

NOTES

1. All but the last term are mentioned in Sam Moskowitz's "How Science Fiction Got Its Name"—still the best discussion of the subject. I once noticed the term *scientific novel* in a 1920s magazine advertisement for S. Fowler Wright's *The Amphibian*; undoubtedly there were other short-lived terms.

2. One of Gernsback's defenses came after the fact, in response to readers' criticisms of the science in Murray Leinster's "The Runaway Skyscraper":

> a writer of scientifiction is privileged to use poetic license, the same as is the writer of any other story. There is rarely a story of this type so perfect as to pass muster with all of its facts, the general theme, and many other points .... [A]uthors often take poetic license, sometimes disregarding the scientific facts, although still retaining enough scientific accuracy to make the plot or story seem probable and at the same time interesting. ("Plausibility in Scientifiction" 675)

Gernsback thus conceded that some stories may have only a limited degree of "scientific accuracy." Later, facing the formidable task of explaining his reprinting of A. Merritt's popular—and distinctly unscientific—*The Moon Pool*, Gernsback tried to forestall criticism with a special editorial defense:

> In the story by A. Merritt in the current issue, the author has hit upon a most extraordinary invention, which, as you will find, he calls "The Shining One." Here is really a new thought, because "The Shining One" is neither a human being, nor a god, nor is it electricity, yet it is possessed of some intelligence. Very strange and fascinating, and most exciting. At first thought you might feel that a story of this kind, while highly interesting, really should be classed with fairy tales. You will, however, soon discover your error, because, after all, the thing is not really impossible. While "The Shining One" may never become a reality, it is conceivable that such an entity might come into existence at some future time, when we know more about science. ("Amazing Creations" 109)

3. In 1964, both Poul Anderson and Arthur C. Clarke published stories about solar-powered spaceships called "Sunjammer" (Anderson's story is mentioned below);

to avoid confusion, Clarke retitled his story "The Wind from the Sun" in all subsequent publications.

4. In November 1961, speaking of recent British writers, Miller spoke of "the 'new wave'—Tubb, Aldiss, and to get to my point, Kenneth Bulmer and John Brunner" (November 1961 167)—which predates most reports of the term by at least three years. In particular, this contradicts the view given by Harlan Ellison that "Judith Merril's August 1966 book review column in *The Magazine of Fantasy and Science Fiction* went a long way toward codifying the parameters of the revolution and therein in the phrase 'new wave' was used for the first time" (Interview with Jeffrey M. Elliot, *Science Fiction Voices #2* 41). Actually, what Merril talked about in that review was "the New Thing."

5. Miller's reviews, along with reviews by other writers, appeared sporadically in *Astounding Science-Fiction* from 1944 to 1951, entitled "Book Review" or "Book Reviews." Starting in October 1951, Miller wrote a regular column of book reviews called "The Reference Library," which ran continuously (except for an occasional missing month) in *Astounding Science-Fiction* (which became *Analog Science Fact/Science Fiction* in January 1961 and *Analog Science Fiction/Science Fact* in April 1965) until January 1975, following Miller's death in 1974. Subsequent references to Miller reviews after October 1951, in this chapter and later chapters, will simply state the date of publication and page number.

6. While I will attempt to cite all the times Miller used the term *hard science fiction* or a conspicuous variant, I have not bothered to record all the times he used *"straight" science fiction* or *"real" science fiction*.

7. I should note, though, that in numerous reviews in the early 1950s, Miller often employed *hard-shell* as a synonym for *hardcover*. However, the passages I cite here were written after he no longer regularly used the term in that way, and hence may have another meaning.

3

"The Closely Reasoned Technological Story": The Development of the Idea of Hard Science Fiction

Although the importance of his contribution is not always acknowledged, everyone has always known that Hugo Gernsback was the modern creator of the term *science fiction*. Until my own research, however, no one knew that P. Schuyler Miller had created the term *hard science fiction*.

This is not surprising. After all, Gernsback loudly proclaimed the existence of a new category of literature called *scientifiction* in the first issue of a new magazine devoted to such stories and repeatedly proselytized on behalf of the genre. In the 1930s, after switching to the term *science fiction*, he called for the celebration of "Science Fiction Week," launched a letter-writing campaign to persuade Hollywood producers to make more science fiction movies, and in 1934, established the Science Fiction League, the first large fan organization. By involving himself in such visible activities, Gernsback not only originated the idea of science fiction but effectively promoted himself as its originator.

P. Schuyler Miller was a different sort of person, not given to standing on soapboxes. He introduced the term *hard science fiction*, quietly, without fanfare, to describe one of the many books he was reviewing. In his first uses of the term, Miller provided little explanation of what it meant, evidently expecting that his readers could readily understand its meaning. Only in the 1960s, after other people had started using the term, did Miller include comments that could be taken as definitions of hard science fiction. And to my knowledge, Miller never announced that he had invented the term. For all these reasons, his key contribution in this area has been overlooked.

The first time P. Schuyler Miller used the exact term *'hard' science fiction* came in November 1957 while he was discussing the republication of John W. Campbell, Jr.'s 1931 novel *Islands of Space*. The entire paragraph should be quoted, for it shows exactly how the term was introduced—casually, and without an accompanying definition:

John Campbell's book [*Islands of Space*] was written a rather long time ago, as a
sequel to his "Arcot, Wade and Morey" novelettes which Fantasy Press collected in
"The Black Star Passes." It was in the grand old *Amazing [Stories] Quarterly* for
Spring, 1931 ... and believe me, it was a world-beater in those days. Although it has
been carefully modernized, it's old-fashioned now. It is also very characteristic of the
best "hard" science fiction of its day. (143)

Miller apparently did not think much of the term, because he did not use it again
until February 1960, when he said that George O. Smith "has written some of the
best 'hard' science fiction we have—such as his 'Venus Equilateral'" (166). Only
two years later did the term begin to appear regularly in his reviews.

The third reference came when he announced in 1962, "As you can see,
[Clarke's *A Fall of Moondust*] is 'hard' science fiction—the kind that many
scientists and engineers are thinking of when they complain that the current
brand is no good, or isn't even science fiction" (February 1962 163). Now he
employed the term more frequently: he said that Clifford D. Simak's "Limiting
Factor" "is a puzzle story, and a very good one—perhaps the closest to 'hard'
science fiction in the book [*Spectrum*]" (September 1962 155). He asked, "Are
you an engineer who longs wistfully for the 'hard' technical science fiction of a
generation ago—the kind that nobody can write any more, unless it's Hal
Clement? Well, the engineers I know turned handsprings over 'A Fall of
Moondust,' by Arthur C. Clarke" (January 1963 170). In December 1963, he
referred to "'hard' science fiction—the technical kind" (86); and in May 1964, he
commented, "Maybe we're short of the 'hard' technical science fiction of the
early years" (89). One noteworthy aspect of these early references is that Miller
sometimes added the adjective *technical* to the term—perhaps to clarify its
meaning—and he thus linked the subgenre not simply to scientific accuracy but
to complicated discussions of scientific issues that were technical. In the
beginning, then, Miller may have regarded hard science fiction simply as stories
which included such long explanations—as were manifest in Campbell's and
Smith's novels. In later references, other qualities emerge as more important in
making a work hard science fiction.

Beginning in 1965, Miller's comments sometimes offer more information about
the meaning of the term and suggest something more than stories with a lot of
technical discussion. In January he cited Clement's *Close to Critical* as "a prime
example of 'hard' science fiction" (January 1965 87); he called Clement "the
master of 'hard' science fiction," and said "The best science-fiction writers create
such Secondary Worlds and take us inside. They may do it, as Hal Clement has
done in his best stories, Robert Heinlein in most of his, and Arthur C. Clarke and
Frank Herbert with notable success, by building their worlds as carefully as an
architect-builder would do his work" (September 1965 147, 148); and, reviewing

Natives of Space, he said "Hal Clement is the master of the meticulously worked out novel of 'hard' science fiction, in which worlds and beings are constructed out of chemistry, physics, and ingenuity" (October 1965 151). In April 1966, he spoke of "'hard' science fiction stories of the kind Arthur Clarke does best" (146), and in June 1966, after discussing an article by Susan Sontag on science fiction, he commented that she "has—happily—not encountered 'hard' SF, and maybe she never will" (143). In June 1967, he complained that Judith Merril's *11th Annual Edition: The Year's Best S-F* "has less 'hard science' science fiction than ever" (163); in August 1973, he spoke of "all you old Analog readers who insist on 'hard' science fiction" (162); and in June 1971, he claimed that "It's getting harder, these days, to find a good 'hard' science-fiction novel in which technical projection is the core of the story"—though he then said that Theodore L. Thomas and Kate Wilhelm's *The Year of the Cloud* "is one" of them (172).

Speaking of other particular writers and works, Miller labelled Dean McLaughlin's "The Permanent Implosion" and Anderson's "Sunjammer" "a pair of 'hard' science-fiction yarns" that "will take you back to the 'Good Old Days' of George O. Smith's 'Venus Equilateral' and Jack Williamson's 'Seetee' stories" (December 1966 160-161); Michael Crichton's *The Andromeda Strain* "is 'hard' science fiction of the kind John Campbell made the trademark of Astounding and Analog" (September 1969 159); he said that Clement's "'Mission of Gravity' is, of course, perhaps the greatest 'hard' SF story ever written" (June 1970 169); Larry Niven's "Neutron Star" was "'hard' science fiction" (February 1972 173); J. Barrington Bayley's "Escape from City 5" "combines 'hard SF' with the experimental techniques" (June 1972 167); Niven's "Inconstant Moon" is "a lovely 'hard SF' story" (May 1973 170); and Keith Laumer "can write science fiction that is just as tight and hard as anyone's" (January 1973 165). In January 1974, he said that James Tiptree, Jr. [Alice Sheldon] "uses plots, themes and formulas that the critics have assured us were given the *coup de grace* by Doc Smith and converted them into dazzling new science fiction—'hard' SF, farcical SF, moving SF, whatever kind of SF amuses him at the moment" and later listed Tiptree's "The Snows Are Melted, the Snows Are Gone," "The Peacefulness of Vivyan," "Mother in the Sky with Diamonds," "The Man Who Walked Home," and "Forever to a Hudson Bay Blanket" as "the 'straight' or 'hard' SF stories" (January 1974 152, 153). And in March 1974, he said that Clarke's *Rendezvous with Rama* "is the kind of 'hard' science fiction that is not likely to appeal to the people who were fascinated by the final part of '2001'" (169). Even without drawing overt attention to the category, Miller's repeated uses of the term in these various reviews clearly played an important role in popularizing the idea of hard science fiction.

The next critic who regularly employed the term was James Blish; indeed, Poul Anderson has attributed to him the claim that he coined the term.[1] In

August 1962, writing as William Atheling, Jr., Blish said, "Dean McLaughlin ... is almost alone among the latest generation in being a writer of 'hard' science fiction. (In the preceding generation there are three—[Algis] Budrys, [Gordon R.] Dickson, and [Randall] Garrett—but of these, Budrys is a law unto himself, and Garrett has spent much of his career in what seems to me to be a deliberate campaign to throw away all his virtues except his industry)" ("The Fens Revisited" 109). Blish, incidentally, may be the first person to use the term without quotation marks, for he later said in the same review that "I can only pray that Dean will ... get back to writing hard science fiction" (112). Later, he used the term a number of times:

Wells used the term [science-fantasy] originally to cover what we would today call "hard" science fiction, in which a conscientious attempt to be faithful to already known facts (as of the date of writing) was the substrate on which the story was to be built .... [Wells] kept his text as "hard" as any purist who also demands good fiction of a fiction-writer could demand .... American science fiction [of the 1940s] was almost entirely "hard"; the best writers of that decade tried to be as respectful of the facts as Wells had been ....

To hitch the word "science" to [fantasies] cannot but be downright offensive to the scientific imagination ... and at best is claiming a cachet to which even the "hard" science-fiction writer has only the most dubious claims (because not one science-fiction story in several thousand involves anything closer to science than minor technological innovations). ("Science-Fantasy and Translations" 99, 101, 103, 106-107)

And in an August 1970 review for *The Magazine of Fantasy and Science Fiction*, Blish said that Julius Fast's *The League of Grey-Eyed Women* "is pure, hard science-fiction" ("Books" 59).

Throughout the 1960s and early 1970s, one sees other commentators starting to use the expression. Harlan Ellison's 1966 "Introduction" to Niven's "The Jigsaw Man" in *Dangerous Visions* observed that Niven "writes what is called 'hard' science fiction—i.e., his scientific extrapolation is based solidly in what is known at the date of his writing" (70).

In his contribution to Judith Merril's June 1966 book review column for *The Magazine of Fantasy and Science Fiction*, Fritz Leiber said that Brian Aldiss's anthology *Yet More Penguin Science Fiction Stories* "is built around a core of 'hard' sf stories—highly imaginative tales bastioned by a wealth of technical fact" and listed as examples James Blish's "Common Time," John Brunner's "The Windows of Heaven," Arthur C. Clarke's "Before Eden," A. Bertram Chandler's "The Cage," Damon Knight's "The Country of the Kind," and Walter M. Miller, Jr.'s "We Made You." Of another anthology, Kingsley Amis and Robert Conquest's *Spectrum IV*, Leiber then commented, "Some 'hard' sf in this fine anthology too," citing Hal Clement's "Hot Planet" and Allen Danzig's "The Great

Nebraska Sea" ("Books" 39).

A year later, Algis Budrys observed that "Arthur C. Clarke, educated and intelligent, is supposed to be one of the big guns in 'hard' science fiction .... [H]e is in fact the author of a clutch of mystical novels and only one or two 'hard' ones" ("October 1967" 123). In 1969, Budrys called Kate Wilhelm's "The Mile-Long Spaceship" "a piece of hard science fiction" ("March 1969" 203), and a decade later, he said that Jerry Pournelle "delivers something less superscientific but closer to what 'hard' science fiction readers are known to like" ("Books" 27).

Donald A. Wollheim and Terry Carr's 1969 blurb to "Kyrie" said, "Poul Anderson is most generally regarded as the best practicing writer of 'hard' science fiction: stories built around careful extrapolation of scientific laws as we understand them today" (*World's Best Science Fiction 1969* 33).

Two years later, John W. Campbell, Jr., called three of H. G. Wells's novels "the 'hard' science fiction of their day" and went on to say that "'Dune' was hard science-fiction worked out in meticulous detail, while 'Dune Messiah' was heavily dominated by a mystical air. Clement's 'Mission of Gravity' and Asimov's 'Foundation' and 'Robot' stories were hard science fiction" (Letter to Jack Williamson 592-593).

In 1971, Isaac Asimov wrote:

For the last dozen years or so, what we might call "hard science fiction" has receded somewhat into the background. By hard science fiction, I mean those stories in which the details of science play an important role and in which the author is accurate about those details, too, and takes the trouble to explain them clearly.

In its place, there has moved into the forefront the emotional story in which science is relegated to the background. Literary style, not physical theory, is what counts; experimentation in form, not in the laboratory .... As for myself (for I will conceal nothing from you) I'm a hard science fiction man myself. For instance, in the same issue of the same magazine in which Harlan Ellison published "I Have No Mouth and I Must Scream," which was all emotion and which won a Hugo, I published "Billiard Ball" which was all thought and which didn't win a Hugo .... I feel better when it turns out that there are still hard science fiction writers among the younger generation. Ben Bova, for instance, writes hard science fiction, and so does Larry Niven. (Introduction to "Neutron Star" 299)

By the 1970s, use of the term had become relatively common. In his 1976 essay "Hard Sciences and Tough Technologies," discussing "approaches" (43) to writing hard science fiction, Hal Clement called Robert A. Heinlein's *Beyond This Horizon* "one of the best examples" (44), praised Murray Leinster's "The Racketeer Ray" (44), and also cited Isaac Asimov, Larry Niven and Poul Anderson as hard science fiction writers (42); and a year later, he called Niven and Anderson "hard science fiction types, as close to the old style space opera as you can get" (Interview with Darrell Schweitzer 51). In 1976, Norman Spinrad noted that "Larry Niven, Hal Clement, Murray Leinster, John W. Campbell, Jr., among others, are generally considered hard science fiction writers. In addition, certain works of writers like Poul Anderson, James Blish, Lester del Rey, Isaac Asimov, and Arthur C. Clarke are also considered hard science fiction" ("Rubber Sciences" 65). The first edition of Neil Barron's bibliography *Anatomy of Wonder* (1976) used the term a number of times: Anderson's *Tau Zero* was "[i]n two ways, an archetypal 'hard' SF novel" (132); Ben Bova's *As on a Darkling Plain* was "an entertaining 'hard' SF tale" and in Bova's "Stars, Won't You Hide Me?" "[h]ard SF and morality plays mingle" (148, 149); the stories in Heinlein's *The Past through Tomorrow* were "hard SF" (197); the stories in Niven's *Neutron Star* were "[e]xcellent hard SF" (232); Christopher Priest's *The Inverted World* was "[w]ell-written hard SF" (239); the stories in Asimov's anthology *Where Do We Go from Here?* "lean toward the 'hard' SF tradition" (286); and Arthur W. Ballou's juvenile *Bound for Mars* was "highly recommended for hard science fiction devotees" (310). In 1978, George S. Elrick's *Science Fiction Handbook for Readers and Writers*, after noting that "any science fiction novel ... can be tagged 'hard' or 'soft,'" offered this definition: "Hard science fiction is basically based on physics, chemistry, biology, astronomy, geology, or mathematics. Example: Hal Clement's *Mission of Gravity*" (6). In 1980, Barry Malzberg, predicting future trends in science fiction, observed, "'Hard' or technologically rigorous work will occupy the same small corner of the market that 'literary' science fiction does now" ("SF Forever" 165).

Well after *hard science fiction* appeared, a variant term emerged: *hard-core science fiction*. To my knowledge, Judith Merril was the first to use that expression. While her 1965 phrase "hard-core science-fiction fan" ("Books," *The Magazine of Fantasy and Science Fiction*, October 1965 98) was ambiguous— "hard-core" could refer either to "science-fiction" or to "fan"—the term is clearly employed in her 1967 anthology: "Within the wide spread of contemporary 'nonrealistic' prose, there does remain a discrete discipline—'hard-core science fiction'—with specialized, and rather demanding parameters. It is no easier to define now than it was in the days of its glory, but it is readily recognizable—and dearly beloved—by those who, like myself, have identified most of their adult intellectual lives with it" (*SF 12* 135-136). And Merril evidently continued to use the term: in the Second Trial Issue of *Locus* in 1968, an anonymous report on a conference about "The Secondary Universe" said that speaker Judith Merril "advanced her thesis that everything from fairy tales to hard-core sf is today considered to be 'science fiction'" ("The Secondary Universe" [1]).

By the late 1960s, a few other commentators were starting to employ this term. Brian W. Aldiss complains in *The Shape of Further Things*, written in 1969 and published in 1970, that "I suffer from the label 'science fiction writer', which allows the *Times Literary Supplement* to toss one of my speculative novels, *Report on Probability A*, to a hard-core SF man, who savages it for not being hard-core SF!" (25-26). Aldiss later comments that Tom Boardman's "publishing firm was bringing out some good hard-core sf" (111). On the cover of the original paperback edition of *Ringworld* in 1970, Larry Niven is called "a hardcore science fiction writer." And Miller employed the term once, in September 1971, when he said that "most [stories in Hans Stefan Santesson's *Crime Prevention in the 30th Century*] are by 'hard core' science fiction writers," though he did not identify those writers by name (165).

By the mid-1970s, this term, like hard science fiction, had become fairly common. In 1974, Thomas M. Scortia said that "The closely reasoned technological story has come to be known as a 'hard-core science fiction story.' Robert A. Heinlein and Dr. Isaac Asimov have long been the leading adepts of this difficult subspecies. More recently, Larry Niven in *Ringworld* and Frank Herbert in *Dragon in the Sea* and the monumental *Dune* have shown themselves masters of the difficult art of constructing a story line that adheres to an internally consistent technical or social structure." Then, making the point that "[t]echnical slips in logic and extrapolation do appear in the best of the hard-core science fiction stories," he cited W. Grey Walter's *The Curve of the Snowflake* as an example ("Science Fiction as the Imaginary Experiment" 139, 140). Elsewhere in the same anthology, Reginald Bretnor asked, "[H]ow many writers, comparatively, have even attempted to explore science fictional alternatives, detours away from Armageddon? A few only, mostly in hard-core sf" ("Science Fiction in the Age of Space" 170); and Jack Williamson spoke of "hard-core science fiction, excepting stories of adventure or fantasy or mood or character," which is "an idea story which usually explores some major human problem" ("Short Stories and Novelettes" 199). Also in 1976, Thomas M. Disch offered this rather more critical definition of the form:

[M]any of the elder statesmen of the field .... would allow writers to deal speculatively with whatever materials might be introduced into a beginning course in the physical sciences, while disbarring irony, aesthetic novelty, any assumption that the readers shares in, or knows about, the civilisation he is riding along in, or even a tone of voice suggesting mature thoughtfulness. SF obeying these rules is called hard-core SF, and some purists would have it that it is the only kind that matters.

And he went on to call Tom Godwin's "The Cold Equations" "a classic hard-core story" ("The Embarrassments of Science Fiction" 143). Barron's *Anatomy of Wonder* occasionally uses this term: Jules Verne's "celebration of the new technology for its own sake" was an "affirmation which characterizes much of the so-called 'hard core' science fiction" (75), and Clement's *Mission of Gravity* was "[c]onsummately logical 'hard core SF'" (167).

A year later, Ben Bova commented, "A lot of things called science fiction will degenerate and ultimately blow away, especially the vapid movies and television shows that are currently getting so much publicity. This is nothing new, and I don't think it will affect the 'hard core' of science fiction" ("Inside *Analog*" 9). In 1978, responding to a reader who praised *Isaac Asimov's Science Fiction Magazine* for featuring "the 'hard-core science fiction,'" Isaac Asimov answered, "I wonder if someone can suggest a better name for the kind of science men like Arthur Clarke, Hal Clement and I write" (cited in Bainbridge 61). And, by the 1980s, some seem to consider this the preferred expression. For example, in the 1986 critical anthology *Hard Science Fiction*, both Robert L. Forward's and John Huntington's essays began with references to, respectively, *hardcore* and *Hard-Core* science fiction.[2]

The term *hardcore* suggests an analogy not to the hard sciences but to pornography. That is, as sexual content is the primary attraction in pornography, scientific content is the primary attraction in science fiction; and, as works with the most and the most explicit sex are labeled *hardcore*, works with the most and the most explicit science are labeled *hardcore science fiction*. Budrys noted the phrase on the cover of *Ringworld* and made the connection explicit: "Inasmuch as Ballantine originally popularized the term 'hard-core pornography,' we don't even have to ask what the term 'hard-core science fiction' may be intended to mean" ("March 1971" 296). Unlike *hard science fiction*, therefore, *hardcore science fiction* has an argument embedded in it, one that could be either supportive—as it implies its emphasis on science makes it central to the genre (an attitude I discuss below)—or critical—as it implies the form's excessive interest in science may be rather perverse or unsavory. Still, since the more neutral term *hard science fiction* came first, and since *hardcore science fiction* was a later adaptation of that term, the implicit intent some later critics attribute to the subgenre—an effort to seize control of the center or *core* of science fiction—was not the initial impulse behind the creation of the term; and, in fact, efforts to ascribe this intent to hard science fiction could be described as false etymology.

As an odd sidelight worth noting, in the late 1960s, just when *hard science fiction* was becoming the standard term, Miller himself, after reading Hal Clement's *Small Changes*, became enamored of another term—*quantitative science fiction*. Finding a version of the phrase in the book, Miller wrote, "Hal Clement is probably our foremost exemplar of *quantitative thought* in science fiction. And this is the key to the best of the 'hard' science fiction with which Clement—and Analog—have been identified" (June 1969 160); later in the same review, he commented, "Quantitative stories are one of the types that are branded as 'Analog' stories, and have been since the days of George O. Smith and 'Venus Equilateral'" (161). Subsequent references include: Poul Anderson's "Brake" "is some of that quantitative science fiction that Hal Clement does so well" (April

1970 169); Anderson's *Tales of the Flying Mountains* "shows his ability to combine 'quantitative' science fiction with action and human problems" (January 1972 169); *Mission of Gravity* "represents the peak of 'quantitative' science fiction" (April 1972 168); Alan E. Nourse's "In Sheep's Clothing" "gives us a 'quantitative' treatment of the gimmick in [John Wyndham's] 'Midwich Cuckoos'" (March 1973 166); Clement "writes 'quantitative' science fiction of a kind that almost no other writer now does" (November 1973 169); and Fritz Leiber's "Kindergarten" "is a kind of quantitative SF" (July 1974 161). It is curious to see Miller, late in life, apparently retreating from a term he himself had developed and popularized; but by the time Miller started to refer to *quantitative science fiction*, *hard science fiction* and *hard core science fiction* were well established, and no one else to my knowledge ever spoke of *quantitative science fiction*.

Looking at overall patterns of usage in the 1960s and 1970s, as listed in Table 1, one finds that this no doubt incomplete survey of the critical literature suggests two trends: first, even in the early years, some commentators seemed to be using the term in a rather expansive manner in reference to authors and texts that do not seem closely tied to the form. Second, however, if one considers only those authors *who are identified as hard science fiction writers by more than one commentator*, a rather limited list of prominent authors emerges—H. G. Wells, Murray Leinster, John W. Campbell, Jr., Robert A. Heinlein, Isaac Asimov, Arthur C. Clarke, Hal Clement, Frank Herbert, James Blish, Poul Anderson, Dean McLaughlin, Larry Niven, Ben Bova, and Kate Wilhelm—suggesting that *consensus* choices for hard science fiction writers tended to be limited to only a small number of authors.

There is also an intriguing chronological pattern in these early designations. Of the fourteen consensus choices, there is one venerable ancestor, Wells; two authors primarily of the 1930s, Campbell and Leinster; two authors associated with Campbell's "Golden Age" of the 1940s, Asimov and Heinlein; six authors who became prominent in the 1950s, Anderson, Blish, Clarke, Clement, Herbert, and McLaughlin; and three authors of the 1960s, Bova, Niven, and Wilhelm. A similar distribution is seen in the other authors designated by only one commentator: Verne, another venerable ancestor; Williamson, primarily of the 1930s; Chandler, del Rey, Fyfe, Simak, and Smith, primarily of the 1940s; Budrys, Dickson, Garrett, Godwin, Knight, Miller, and Walter, primarily of the 1950s; and Ballou, Bayley, Brunner, Crichton, Danzig, Fast, Laumer, Priest, Thomas, and Tiptree, primarily of the 1960s.[3] Overall, nine of the fourteen authors called hard science fiction writers by consensus, and twenty-six of all the thirty-eight authors called hard science fiction writers, are predominantly associated with the 1950s and 1960s. This is worth noting because, as already seen and as discussed below, many of these commentators wish to see hard science fiction as an older form, dating back to the 1940s or even earlier; however, *the majority of their references involve more modern authors*.[4]

Other interesting aspects of these early usages include: In all of these early uses of the expression, the commentators do not claim to be originating the term; the term *hard* is with rare exceptions in quotation marks, suggesting the writers regard the term as slang;[5] and writers often define the term while using it, indicating that they do not expect readers to understand the term without explanation. A possible explanation would be that these commentators were picking up the term not directly from Miller's columns but from conversations between science fiction writers and fans who were either influenced by Miller or who independently developed the term; thus, *hard science fiction* may have retained quotation marks to mark its possible origin in conversation. Also, the term clearly stems from the expression *hard science*, although the expression *hard shell* may also have been a contributing factor. Another possible—and more prosaic—influence may simply have been that stories of this type, filled with detailed scientific descriptions, were hard to read, especially for readers who lacked a background in science.

Finally, it might be worthwhile to compile various statements from this time that could be taken as definitions of hard science fiction:

1. The meticulously worked out novel of "hard" science fiction, in which worlds and beings are constructed out of chemistry, physics, and ingenuity .... a good "hard" science fiction novel in which technical projection is the core of the story (Miller, October 1965 151; June 1971 172);

2. "Hard" science fiction, in which a conscientious attempt to be faithful to already known facts (as of the date of writing) was the substrate on which the story was to be built (Blish, "Science-Fantasy and Translations" 99);

3. "Hard" science fiction—i.e., [where] scientific extrapolation is based solidly in what is known at the date of his writing (Ellison, "Introduction" to "The Jigsaw Man" 70);

4. "Hard" sf stories—highly imaginative tales bastioned by a wealth of technical fact (Leiber, "Books" 39);

5. "Hard" science fiction: stories built around careful extrapolation of scientific laws as we understand them today (Wollheim and Carr, *World's Best Science Fiction 1969* 33);

6. By hard science fiction, I mean those stories in which the details of science play an important role and in which the author is accurate about those details, too, and takes the trouble to explain them clearly. (Asimov, Introduction to "Neutron Star" 299)

In all these statements, three characteristic traits emerge: Hard science fiction is *scientifically accurate* according to the knowledge of its day; hard science fiction includes *explanations and presentations* of its scientific facts; and hard science fiction is based on *careful extrapolation*, or scientific thinking, from known facts to speculations.

So defined, hard science fiction might be regarded as a fairly small and recognizable part of modern science fiction; however, by the mid-1970s, more formal works of criticism started to discuss the subgenre, and in those hands, the concept of hard science fiction seemed to expand more radically.

Previous commentators, as observed, generally applied the term *hard science fiction* with some selectivity to a small number of authors; however, the new tendency among academic critics in the 1970s was to establish *hard science fiction* as one of a few broad categories encompassing the entire genre. One early effort of this kind came in the 1973 *Cliffs Notes* edition of *Science Fiction: An Introduction*, by L. David Allen of the University of Nebraska. According to Allen, "Hard Science Fiction" was "science fiction in which the major impetus for the exploration which takes place is one of the so-called hard, or physical, sciences, including chemistry, physics, biology, astronomy, geology, and possibly mathematics, as well as the technology associated with, or growing out of, one of those sciences" (5). In Allen's view, hard science fiction constituted one of the four basic types of science fiction, the others being "Soft Science Fiction," "Science Fantasy," and "Fantasy" (5-7). He further described Jules Verne as "the archetypal practitioner of Extrapolative Hard Science Fiction"; Hal Clement was "the best and most consistent descendent from Verne" (13), and Clement's *Mission of Gravity* was "one of the very best examples of extrapolative hard science fiction available" (62).

In later academic works, hard science fiction was used in a similarly expansive manner to refer to virtually all forms of science fiction that predated the New Wave movement of the 1960s, or to all new works that were reminiscent of earlier eras. Thus, in 1979, Peter Nicholls's *The Science Fiction Encyclopedia* offered this broad definition of *hardcore sf*: "first ... the kind of sf which repeats the themes and usually the style of genre sf written during the so-called Golden Age of SF; second, it is sf that deals with the so-called 'hard' sciences" ("Hardcore SF" 273). In the second edition of this reference work (*The Encyclopedia of Science Fiction*, edited by John Clute and Peter Nicholls), Nicholls interestingly expands on this definition in an entry now entitled "Hard SF." Nicholls attempts to establish a distinction between *hardcore sf*, "the kind of sf that repeats the themes and (to a degree) the style of the genre sf written during the so-called Golden Age of SF," and *hard sf*, which is (quoting Allan Steele) "a form of imaginative literature that uses either established or carefully extrapolated science as its backbone" (542). To say the least, this is not a distinction that can be observed in uses of the term during the last twenty-five years, where *hardcore science fiction* and *hard science fiction* are generally used interchangeably; rather, it seems an after-the-fact distinction introduced by Nicholls to logically justify use of both terms.

There is also an implicit expansiveness in Darko Suvin's use of the term in *Metamorphoses of Science Fiction* (1979): Edgar Allan Poe's "influence encompasses on the one hand the mechanical marvels of Verne and the dime-novels, and on the other the escapist strain in some of the 'hardest' U.S. SF, for example, Robert A. Heinlein's time-traveling solipsism" (143).

In 1982, Donald M. Hassler's *Comic Tones in Science Fiction* began by equating "the pulp literature genre" with "hard science fiction" (8) in the manner of Nicholls, then unhesitatingly labelled Frederik Pohl a hard science fiction writer, even while acknowledging his lack of scientific training, on the grounds that both Clement and Pohl "stay close in their writing to the hard analysis of conditions and givens as modern science sees them" (103), a rather loose standard. Another passage in Hassler's book implies that Theodore Sturgeon is also a hard science fiction writer: "Significantly, Clement and Pohl have survived (along with Asimov, Sturgeon, and some others) and are still creating this effect forty years after Campbell took over *Astounding* when 'softer' writers have moved on to other things" (103-104). Also in 1982, Hassler's *Hal Clement* speaks of *Astounding Science-Fiction* in 1944 as "the leading pulp magazine for hard science fiction" (8).

Carol McGuirk, citing Nicholls's 1979 definition as evidence, announces, "The only uncontested shift of consensus in SF history seems to have been the first: the displacement of space opera by hard science fiction shortly before World War II" and lists Heinlein, Asimov and Sturgeon as the "first impetus" behind hard science fiction ("The 'New' Romancers" 111).

As an indication of ongoing efforts to further expand the meaning of the term, George Slusser and Eric S. Rabkin's 1986 critical anthology *Hard Science Fiction* included entire essays on the eighteenth-century geologist Thomas Burnet, William Morris, and C. S. Lewis, along with two essays on Stanislaw Lem; Gregory Benford's "Is There a Technological Fix for the Human Condition?" conditionally brought Lem, Olaf Stapledon, Brian W. Aldiss and Rudy Rucker into the fold; Frank McConnell's "Sturgeon's Law: First Corollary" calls Stapledon's *Star Maker* "the hardest of hard SF stories" (22); George Slusser's "The Ideal Worlds of Science Fiction" focuses on John W. Campbell, Jr.'s "Who Goes There?" and Isaac Asimov's Foundation trilogy as exemplars of the form; and James Gunn's "The Readers of Hard Science Fiction" incorporated works like A. E. van Vogt's *The Voyage of the Space Beagle*, Ursula K. Le Guin's *The Left Hand of Darkness*, Bob Shaw's *Orbitsville*, Jack Vance's *The Languages of Pao*, Samuel R. Delany's *Babel-17*, and John Brunner's *Stand on Zanzibar*, *The Jagged Orbit*, *The Sheep Look Up*, and *The Shockwave Rider*.

As one example of the apparent logic behind these massive territorial grabs, consider Michael Collings's "Science and Scientism in C. S. Lewis's *That Hideous Strength*." Collings begins by acknowledging the obvious—"On the surface, it seems strange to discuss C. S. Lewis's *That Hideous Strength* in the context of 'Hard Core Science Fiction'" (131)—but goes on to say that the novel "interweaves scientific jargon and technical explanation," "focuses on variations of scientific procedure, purposes, and applications," "employs the language of science and science fiction," "uses the scientific method as a means of defining and identifying the extrahuman beings function in the novels," and "makes a single assumption about the nature of the physical universe and then proceeds to explore the workings of scientific observation and experimentation in that universe" (133, 135, 139); and he concludes that the novel "is, in its emphasis on science as a unifying element in the novel, closely related in technique and function to traditional hard science fiction novels" (140). In sum, it seems Collings's opinion is that *hard science fiction* includes all writers whose knowledge and use of science exceeds the puerile.

As an interesting snapshot of the perceptions of modern science fiction readers, the data compiled by William Bainbridge in *Dimensions of Science Fiction* suggest that the meaning of the term *hard science fiction* has also broadened somewhat in the community of science fiction fans. Based on a factor analysis of responses from a survey of almost 600 science fiction fans, Bainbridge concluded that at least twenty-seven writers could be confidently labeled *hard science authors*, including some more or less predictable names— Asimov, Dickson, Clement, Pournelle, Anderson, Niven, Clarke, Campbell, Bova, Heinlein and Blish; some figures hitherto regarded as marginal—Leinster, del Rey, Simak, Fred Hoyle, and Pohl; and some names rarely if ever associated with the subgenre—Jack Williamson, Harry Harrison, E. E. Smith, A. E. van Vogt, Mack Reynolds, Keith Laumer, Donald A. Wollheim, Lin Carter, Spider Robinson, Joe Haldeman, and L. Sprague de Camp. Bainbridge's overall conlusion is that there are three basic categories of science fiction—hard science, new wave, and fantasy—which together constitute the entire genre.[6]

Finally, the most recent effort to establish the nature of hard science fiction—David G. Hartwell and Kathryn Cramer's 1994 anthology *The Ascent of Wonder: The Evolution of Hard Science Fiction*—also drifts toward eclecticism. In extensive introductory comments justifying the inclusion of some less than obvious choices—for example, stories by Edgar Allan Poe, Nathaniel Hawthorne, Rudyard Kipling, Miles J. Breuer, Clifford D. Simak, J. G. Ballard, Ursula K. Le Guin, and John Sladek—the editors offer several defining criteria for hard science fiction. At times, it is purely based on subject matter: All stories about scientists at work, for example, automatically qualify as hard science fiction. At times, it is determined by a writing process: All writers who follow H. G. Wells's dictum—to take one new idea and explore all its ramifications—produce hard science fiction, even if their method of development is not exactly scientific. At times, it is a matter of characteristic narrative form: Works of hard science fiction tend to feature certain types of characters—strong-minded, practical men and women—and certain types of stories—problems are solved, catastrophes are survived, and so on. At times, it involves a certain authorial philosophy, the hard science fiction "attitude"—that everything in the universe is ultimately knowable and its difficulties surmountable. At times, it involves a certain atmosphere, or mood, the hard science fiction "affect." Finally, stories that lack any or all of these traits may qualify as hard science fiction if they seem to respond to or comment on other hard science fiction texts. Since there are few science fiction stories that fail to meet one of these criteria, it is clear that, in the hands of Hartwell and Cramer, *hard science fiction* almost becomes a synonym for *science fiction*.

Such efforts to broaden the term were not unopposed; in his review of the anthology *Hard Science Fiction* in *Extrapolation*, David Samuelson asserted that many papers were "related only peripherally to hard science fiction" and that "[i]nstead of Burnet, Morris, Lewis, and Lem, however, Clarke, Clement, Benford and Brunner might be studied at length, with due consideration to Verne and Wells, if not Asimov or Heinlein, 'for historical reasons'" (358, 360). Samuelson thus seems to argue for a more traditional and limited meaning for *hard science fiction*. Reviewing *The Ascent of Wonder* in *Locus*, Gary K. Wolfe found the volume not properly focused on hard science fiction, complaining of its "unlikely candidates" and maintaining that the anthology presents "a fuzzy set with a clear center and no boundaries at all—there's no principle of exclusion, no acknowledgement that any subset of sf exists *other* than hard sf. In other words, there's a fair amount of fudging going on here ... sf readers who hope to clarify their understanding of hard sf aren't likely to find much illumination coming from the very fuzzy set of stories included here" (19, 21). In his review of the anthology, Samuelson complained that "its scatter-shot methods of selection and presentation in fact deprecate the real thing, watering it down so much as to virtually destroy any generic consistency" ("A Softening of the Hard-Sf Concept" 409).[7] Another academic critic who sought a narrower definition was Patrick Parrinder, who said in *Science Fiction: Its Teaching and Criticism* that

'Hard' SF is related to 'hard facts' and also to the 'hard' or engineering sciences. It does not necessarily entail realistic speculation about a future world, although its bias is undoubtedly realistic. Rather, this is the sort of SF that most appeals to scientists themselves—and is often written by them. The typical 'hard' SF writer looks for new and unfamiliar scientific theories and discoveries which could provide the occasion for a story, and, at its more didactic extreme, the story is only a framework for introducing the scientific concept to the reader. (14-15)

While his is not a sympathetic definition, Parrinder is at least limiting the term to something resembling its original sense.

Some writers who fit the established label of hard science fiction have indicated that they wish the meaning of the term to remain restricted. In 1976, Hal Clement spoke of "the rather narrow limits of 'hard' science fiction" ("The Creation of Imaginary Beings" 260); in his 1979 interview with Jeffrey M. Elliot, Poul Anderson pointedly called himself "one of the comparatively few people in the field who writes what is called 'hard' science fiction" (*Science Fiction Voices #2* 43); and in his 1981 "Introduction" to Orson Scott Card's *Unaccompanied Sonata*, Ben Bova described "the narrow spectrum of readers who want nothing more than 'hard-core' science fiction" (18). More recently, in his 1994 introduction to *The Ascent of Wonder*, Gregory Benford says that "some have tried to appropriate the hard sf name for any narrative which nods, however slightly, toward science at all. (J. G. Ballard, Ursula K. Le Guin and Gene Wolfe, for example, do not feature on the hard sf fan's list, but they have been enlisted in the corps by some)" (15); of course, Benford's complaint had to be phrased diplomatically, since the anthology he was introducing offered three stories by two of the dubiously included authors he names.

A recent exchange of letters in *Science Fiction Eye* also suggests that modern hard science fiction writers are continuing to resist the efforts to expand the term. In the ninth issue, Luke McGuff, "with assist from Jane Hawkins and Vonda N. McIntyre," condemned Charles Sheffield for "defining hard SF using the sheet metal icons of the Campbell era" and maintained that "Authors such as Vonda N. McIntyre, Janet Kagan, Octavia Butler, C. J. Cherryh, Pat Cadigan, Joan Vinge, Alice Sheldon (James Tiptree, Jr.). Joanna Russ, Kate Wilhelm, Ursula K. Le Guin, A. C. Crispin, Sarah Starney, Suzy McKee Charnas, Sharon Baker, and Elizabeth Lynn are hard science fiction writers" because "[t]hey take the science of today and extrapolate it into the future" (Letter, *Science Fiction Eye*, No. 9 10)—which is virtually equivalent to saying that all science fiction writers are hard science fiction writers. In the next issue, Sheffield wrote back to say that such writers clearly do not fit "the generally accepted meaning" of the term, and offered an interesting analogy to explain the logic behind McGuff's effort to expand the term:

Among those fortunate beings who write verse, there are some who write rhyming ballads, and some who write free verse, and some who write limericks.

There are, in fact, some who write *only* limericks. It is not difficult to find out who they are. If everything they produce has a certain rhyming pattern and scans like "There was a young man from Nantucket," they are limerick writers and *only* limerick writers. "Hard limerick writers," we will call them .... Now, suppose that there is a certain cachet to be derived from being thought of as a hard limerick writer .... Then some versifiers, who are not thought of as hard limerick writers, and who perhaps did not start out in life with university training in hard limericks, would probably like to join the group.

What can they do? They can restrict their output to what everyone recognizes as limerick, and hope at some point to be listed among the leading hard limerick writers. That is not easy, because once a balladeer, always a balladeer, at least in the minds of the public.

Or—a much easier solution—our would-be hard limerick writers can get their friends to say, "The old definition of the limerick is dead. Today, and in the future,

the term 'limerick' will also include sonnets, sestinas, triolets, and heroic ballads."
    That is what McGuff wants to do, not to verse but to hard SF .... (Letter, *Science Fiction Eye*, No. 10 4, 3-4)

Thus, just as the limerick is a small and carefully defined form of poetry, Sheffield argues for hard science fiction as a small and carefully defined form of science fiction.[8]
    With all of these efforts to expand the meaning of *hard science fiction* to include a wide variety of previously excluded writers, it was perhaps inevitable that some would propose the existence of an opposing category of *soft science fiction*. The term may have been dimly anticipated in Miller's comment from November 1957, where, as noted, he contrasted Campbell's "hard sell [hard shell]" science fiction with Murray Leinster's "fashionably 'soft' science fiction" (145). But the exact term *soft science fiction* does not appear until the 1970s; as noted, L. David Allen apparently was the first to employ the term, defining "Soft Science Fiction" as

science fiction in which the major impetus for the exploration is one of the so-called soft sciences, that is, sciences focusing on human activities, most of which have not been fully accepted as being as rigorous or as capable of prediction as the physical sciences. Soft Science Fiction would include any stories based on such organized approaches to knowledge such as sociology, psychology, anthropology, political science, historiography, theology, linguistics, and some approaches to myth. (*Science Fiction* 6)

Elrick offered a similar definition in 1978: "Soft science fiction is basically based on sociology, anthropology, political science, theology, or mythology. Example: Brian Aldiss's *Galaxies, Like Grains of Sand* [sic]" (6). A year later, Peter Nicholls explained that soft science fiction was a "not very precise term ... generally applied either to sf which deals with the soft sciences, or to sf which does not deal with recognizable science at all, but emphasizes human feelings" ("Soft SF" 556). Hard science fiction, a term that once described a rather small category of science fiction, was now becoming one of two expansive categories encompassing the entire genre.
    Interestingly, even as commentators announce these two forms of science fiction, they may simultaneously express unhappiness with the classification: Elrick adds that "[b]ecause many novels are both hard *and* soft, classification tends to be ring-around-the-rosie" (6); and Nicholls says in *The Encyclopedia of Science Fiction* that "[t]he contrasting of soft sf with hard sf is sometimes illogical" ("Soft SF" 1131). The notion that this division of science fiction is either impossible or illogical is something to discuss further in a later chapter.
    If one carefully considers the various comments presented so far on the subject, however, hard science fiction does emerge generally as a more cohesive

field of writing with a number of definite traits: an emphasis on scientific accuracy and scientific language, documentary depictions of the near future, and careful scientific extrapolation toward more extravagant creations. And if these traits are accepted as characteristic of the form, it may be possible to restrict use of the term *hard science fiction* to something close to its original meaning.

Still, before reaching any conclusions, there is one other important body of critical commentary that needs to be examined: the writings of some of its major authors describing hard science fiction and the process of writing it.

Table 1. Authors Explicitly Identified as
Hard or Hard-Core Science Fiction Writers by
Popular Commentators in the 1960s and 1970s
(Listed in Chronological Order of First Identification)

Author: Work Identified (if any)	Identifier (Month/Year of Identification)
John W. Campbell, Jr.: *Islands of Space*	Norman Spinrad (76) P. Schuyler Miller (11/57)
George O. Smith: *Venus Equilateral*	Miller (2/60)
Arthur C. Clarke: *A Fall of Moondust* "Before Eden" *Rendezvous with Rama*	Miller (9/65, 4/66); Algis Budrys (10/67); Spinrad (76); Isaac Asimov (78) Miller (2/62, 1/63) Fritz Leiber (6/66) Miller (3/74)
Dean McLaughlin: "The Permanent Implosion"	James Blish (8/62) Miller (12/67)
Algis Budrys	Blish (8/62)
Randall Garrett	Blish (8/62)
Gordon R. Dickson	Blish (8/62)

Clifford D. Simak: "Limiting Factor"	Miller (9/62)
H. G. Wells	Blish (63); John W. Campbell, Jr. (1/71)
Hal Clement:	Miller (5/64, 9/65, 6/69); L. David Allen (73); Spinrad (76); Asimov (78)
Close to Critical	Miller (1/65)
Natives of Space	Miller (10/65)
"Hot Planet"	Leiber (6/66)
Mission of Gravity	Miller (6/70); Campbell (1/71); Allen (73); Neil Barron (76); George S. Elrick (78)
Robert A. Heinlein:	Miller (9/65); Thomas M. Scortia (74); Hal Clement (76)
Beyond This Horizon	Clement (76)
The Past through Tomorrow	Barron (76)
Frank Herbert:	Miller (9/65)
Dune	Campbell (1/71); Scortia (74)
The Dragon in the Sea	Scortia (74)
Larry Niven:	Harlan Ellison (66); Asimov (71); Clement (76,77); Spinrad (76)
"Neutron Star"	Miller (2/72)
Ringworld	Scortia (74)
"Inconstant Moon"	Miller (5/73)
Neutron Star	Barron (76)
James Blish:	Spinrad (76)
"Common Time"	Leiber (6/66)
John Brunner: "The Windows of Heaven"	Leiber (6/66)
H. B. Fyfe: "Protected Species"	Leiber (6/66)
A. Bertram Chandler: "The Cage"	Leiber (6/66)
Damon Knight: "The Country of the Kind"	Leiber (6/66)

Walter M. Miller, Jr.: "We Made You"	Leiber (6/66)
Allen Danzig: "The Great Nebraska Sea"	Leiber (6/66)
Poul Anderson:	Donald A. Wollheim/Terry Carr (69); Clement (76,77); Spinrad (76)
"Sunjammer"	Miller (12/67)
Tau Zero	Barron (76)
Jack Williamson: "Seetee" stories	Miller (12/67)
Kate Wilhelm:	
"The Mile-Long Spaceship"	Budrys (3/69)
The Year of the Cloud	Miller (6/71)
Michael Crichton: *The Andromeda Strain*	Miller (9/69)
Julius Fast: *The League of Grey-Eyed Women*	Blish (8/70)
Theodore L. Thomas: *The Year of the Cloud*	Miller (6/71)
Isaac Asimov:	Asimov (71,78); Scortia (74); Clement (76); Spinrad (76)
Foundation stories	Campbell (1/71)
Robot stories	Campbell (1/71)
"Billiard Ball"	Asimov (71)
Ben Bova:	Asimov (71)
As on a Darkling Plain	Barron (76)
"Stars, Won't You Hide Me?"	Barron (76)
J. Barrington Bayley: "Escape from City 5"	Miller (6/72)
Keith Laumer	Miller (1/73)
Jules Verne	Allen (73)

James Tiptree, Jr. [Alice Sheldon]:	Miller (1/74)
"The Snows Are Melted, the Snows Are Gone"	Miller (1/74)
"The Peacefulness of Vivyan"	Miller (1/74)
"Mother in the Sky with Diamonds"	Miller (1/74)
"The Man Who Walked Home"	Miller (1/74)
"Forever to a Hudson Bay Blanket"	Miller (1/74)

W. Grey Walter: *The Curve of the Snowflake*	Scortia (74)

Murray Leinster:	Spinrad (76)
"The Racketeer Ray"	Clement (76)

Lester del Rey	Spinrad (76)

Tom Godwin: "The Cold Equations"	Thomas M. Disch (76)

Arthur W. Ballou: *Bound for Mars*	Barron (76)

Christopher Priest: *The Inverted World*	Barron (76)

Jerry Pournelle	Budrys (5/79)

NOTES

1. Anderson's comment: "The term itself, 'hard' science fiction, originated with the late James Blish, who, afterward, remarked that his original intention had been greatly misinterpreted" (Interview with Jeffrey M. Elliot, *Science Fiction Voices #2* 42). Since Blish was not noted for making extravagant or self-serving assertions, Anderson's report of his claim to have created *hard science fiction* demands attention. Blish did not specify original places of publication for the reviews published in *The Issue at Hand* and *More Issues at Hand*, and because the pieces were often, as he acknowledged, rewritten for book publication, it is difficult to establish exactly when Blish first used the term without sorting through all of the fanzines where Blish first published. In the case of the quotations cited, Blish says that the comments on McLaughlin originally appeared in August 1962 and the second discussion combined pieces from 1960 and 1963; the passages about hard science fiction in the later piece certainly involve the later date, however, since they start with a reference to an

August 1962 issue of *The Magazine of Fantasy and Science Fiction* and immediately proceed to an attack on Brian W. Aldiss's "Hothouse" stories, published in 1961. Even if Blish's written use of the term dates to 1960, the fact remains that Miller used it earlier.

Of course, exact dates for the first *published* use of the term are not conclusive in themselves. It remains possible that Blish started using the word while speaking at the science fiction conventions both he and Miller attended and that Miller picked up the term from him. It is also possible that they developed the term independently. To explain Blish's claim that he originated the term, my theory would be that he first used the term without thinking about where he had heard it earlier; later, somebody told him that he had been the first to use it; and Blish, lacking knowledge of its true origins, accepted the statement as true.

2. For emphasis, Norman Spinrad once combined the terms: "the true hardcore hard science fiction" ("The Hard Stuff" 103).

3. My classifications are based on when the authors became prominent, not necessarily the date of first publications. Thus, Clarke, Clement, and Blish all published some works in the 1940s, but did not earn recognition as major writers until the 1950s.

4. One might protest that many of these references come from book review columns that naturally focus on more modern works; but this is not always true. Miller diligently noted books published by earlier writers and had many opportunities to call writers like Isaac Asimov, A. E. van Vogt, and Theodore Sturgeon hard science fiction writers, yet he never did.

5. Oddly enough, the term often retained quotation marks for a while. As late as 1974, Anne McCaffrey wrote, "Since we are dealing with science fiction, it would be nice if we could reduce Webster's definition to equations. However, most 'hard' science fiction aficionados would probably quarrel with our algebra" ("Hitch Your Dragon to a Star" 288). Other commentators at this time adopt Blish's convention of employing the quotation marks the first time, then dropping them. Thus, in 1974 Jack Williamson first says Campbell "was featuring 'hard' science fiction in *Analog*" and later says he was "[b]ewildered by the lack of hard science fiction on the required lists—except for a few works by Wells, Hal Clement, and Asimov" ("Science Fiction, Teaching and Criticism" 322). And Lester del Rey's 1979 "Introduction" to *The Best of Hal Clement* begins, "From the beginning, there have been two main divisions of science fiction. One of these is what has come to be called 'hard' science fiction"; but he goes on to say, "Hard science fiction is that branch which tries to stick rigorously to the known facts of the physical sciences" (xi).

6. If seen as a survey of attitudes about science fiction in its community or a mapping of factions in that community, Bainbridge's analysis may be sound; one can object to the notion that these divisions are automatically reflected in the literature of science fiction. The issue is discussed below.

7. Had *The Ascent of Wonder* been available at an earlier stage in my research, I would undoubtedly be discussing the anthology at greater length. In a sense, Wolfe's and Samuelson's criticisms seem harsh; the stories Hartwell and Cramer present are generally good, and they do include virtually every major author prominently identified with hard science fiction. Still, many of their choices can only be described

as idiosyncratic; particularly questionable, I think, is Hartwell's repeated claim that the works of J. G. Ballard represent a distinct strain of hard science fiction. In the course of this study, I provide several reasons for regarding the designation as inappropriate.

To properly appreciate *The Ascent of Wonder*, one should perhaps consider its subtitle: *The Evolution of Hard Science Fiction*. Now, if a biologist is describing the *evolution* of some animal, she might properly discuss not only its direct ancestors but also its more remote ancestors, offshoots, and related species. By analogy, the presence of some stories in this anthology might be justified as a useful part of the story of the *evolution* of hard science fiction; what Wolfe and Samuelson seem to want, and what Hartwell and Cramer do not provide, is an anthology more narrowly focused on the *history* of hard science fiction.

8. Gregory Benford also likens hard science fiction to poetry, but his more dignified choice is the sonnet: "The constraints in science fiction are analogous in many ways to the meter and rhyme of a sonnet. You can't write a sonnet just any way. You can only write it within a very narrow set of constraints" (Interview with Jeffrey M. Elliot, *Science Fiction Voices #3* 47).

4

"Treating the Whole Thing as a Game": Hard Science Fiction as Seen by Its Writers

One characteristic of several writers known as hard science fiction writers is their willingness to talk about their creative process in other forums. In response to John W. Campbell, Jr.'s request, Hal Clement happily wrote "Whirligig World" to further explain the science behind *Mission of Gravity* and later wrote several essays about writing hard science fiction; Poul Anderson has described how he created the imaginary world Cleopatra in the essay "The Creation of Imaginary Worlds" and elsewhere; Robert F. Forward presented a paper at one Eaton Conference about how he developed the background for his novel *Dragon's Egg*, a paper later published in *Hard Science Fiction* as "When Science Writes the Fiction"; Larry Niven talked in great detail about the development of *Ringworld*, *The Mote in God's Eye*, and *The Integral Trees* in *N-Space*; and it is the recent habit of Arthur C. Clarke, Forward, and others to add Afterwords to their novels explaining in detail the scientific data and speculation in those works.

It would seem that the work of hard science fiction writers is similar to the work of scientists in at least one respect: Scientists should always be willing to describe in detail how they performed their experiments, so that others can duplicate and check on their work; and hard science fiction writers always seem willing to describe their imaginative creations in detail, thus opening up their work to the same kind of inspection. Like scientists, of course, writers cannot always be trusted to accurately and completely describe their thought processes; but there are in these self-descriptions some common themes that seem generally relevant to the entire field of hard science fiction.

The first article about a piece of writing firmly identified as hard science fiction, Clement's "Whirligig World," accompanied the first publication of *Mission of Gravity* in *Astounding Science-Fiction* in 1953. In the essay, Clement begins by describing the central preoccupation of the form:

The fun ... lies in treating the whole thing as a game. I've been playing the game since I was a child, so the rules must be quite simple. They are: for the reader of a science-fiction story, they consist of finding as many as possible of the author's statements or implications which conflict with the facts as science currently understands them. For the author, the rule is to make as few such slips as he possibly can. (102)

The idea that this kind of writing is a "game" is subtly reinforced by Clement's decision to describe his planet Mesklin as a "whirligig," a word that can variously mean a top, a pinwheel, or a merry-go-round—all objects associated with children at play.

Other hard science fiction writers have heartily endorsed Clement's metaphor of their work as a game. In 1961, when Hal Clement published a letter in *Analog: Science Fact/Science Fiction* that began, "Been playing 'the game' with Poul Anderson's 'Longest Voyage' in the December [1960] issue," and proceeded to point out a number of possible errors in the story, Anderson's following reply began, "I am delighted that the Game is still being played" ("Brass Tacks" 171, 172). Gregory Benford later argued, "There are virtually no cheat-free stories, including my own, and playing the game of finding the error in the story seems to motivate a lot of students to engage in physics who otherwise sit there and stare" (cited in Huntington, "Hard-Core Science Fiction and the Illusion of Science" 50); and he elsewhere noted, "A reasonable standard, generally shared by most hard SF writers, is that one should not make errors which are visible to the lay reader" ("Is There a Technological Fix for the Human Condition?" 84). In 1989, Forward began his essay on writing hard science fiction by making essentially the same point as Clement: "When writing hardcore science fiction, the purpose is to have the science as accurate as possible and matched to the story ... There are lots of ways to make errors in science fiction stories. The goal is not to make any errors" ("When Science Writes the Fiction" 1). At the same time, Poul Anderson said that

the author .... has thought of the basic idea, worked out the details as logically and thoroughly as possible, described them in a story, and gotten the story into print. Now there it sits, an irresistibly tempting target for anyone who suspects it contains mistakes of either fact or logic. Hal Clement calls this "the game." It is played between author and readers. The author's moves are all made beforehand, with the object of having zero flaws in the construction .... The fewer scientific nits readers can pick, the higher the author scores. ("Nature: Laws and Surprises" 7)

In 1990, Larry Niven notes that "[h]ard science fiction in particular is a game played with the readers. They try to spot my mistakes" ("Foreword" to *N-Space* 25). Recently, Benford even spoke of this process as "the sacred game" ("Real Science, Imaginary Worlds" 23), implying that its principles demand an almost religious respect.

One might begin, then, by noting this principle: Writing hard science fiction can be seen as a game, and the major goal of this game is *to avoid making scientific errors in its stories*. There are four ways to achieve this: Two are noted in "Whirligig World" but rejected as unsatisfactory; a third way is implicit in some stories by Clement and works and comments from other writers later identified as hard science fiction writers; and the fourth way is the subject of Clement's article.

The first way to avoid scientific errors is simply to employ jargon—impressive-sounding double-talk that acknowledges the seeming implausibility of some device without trying to explain it—what Clement called the "gobbledygook subclass" of science fiction ("Hard Sciences and Tough Technologies" 51). This is one way that a story, in Benford's words, can "cheat." In the case of *Mission of Gravity*, Clement describes the problem of Mesklin's enormous gravity and says, "Any science fiction author can get around that .... Simply invent a gravity screen. No one will mind little details like violation of the law of conservation of energy, or the difference of potential across the screen which will prevent the exchange of anything more concrete than visual signals .... No one but Astounding readers, that is; and there is my own conscience" ("Whirligig World" 106-107). As Clement later conceded, the method does have "obvious advantages"—"the scope of [a writer's] story is not constrained by mere facts; and a vocabulary can serve in place of scientific knowledge" ("Hard Sciences and Tough Technologies" 42).

Clement offers three reasons for avoiding this approach, each involving a different group of science fiction readers. In "Whirligig World," the problem is that terminology alone will not satisfy knowledgeable readers, who presumably are looking for more scientific substance in the science fiction they read. Twenty years later, however, Clement is more concerned about the reactions of people who do not regularly read science fiction: Gobbledygook "furnishes ammunition to intellectual snobs who can't admit that science fiction is a legitimate branch of the storyteller's art" ("Hard Sciences and Tough Technologies" 42). The major reason, however, seems to involve only one reader—the writer—as indicated by Clement's reference to his "conscience": The true author of hard science fiction regards the use of obfuscatory jargon as a type of cheating, not doing the work of science fiction; it does not provide what he called in the same essay the necessary "discipline" of hard science fiction (45).[1]

The second way to avoid scientific errors is to speculate in an area where there is little scientific knowledge. While writing *Mission of Gravity* in 1953, for example, Clement said, "I don't have to describe the life processes [of Mesklinites] in rigorous detail. Anyone who wants me to will have to wait until someone can do the same with our own life form" (113).[2] Still, though Clement would venture into vague or questionable science as a small part of his writing, he did not wish to focus a story in these areas of scientific unknowns: As he said in 1979, "There may be an afterlife. Telepathy and other psionic manifestations may be real and may some day come under orderly human control. There may be flaws in the laws of thermodynamics, even the first one. It is fun to read stories about such possibilities, but I seem to lack what it takes to write them" ("Author's Afterword" 374). Presumably, writing about matters where one cannot make scientific errors, like inventing a few terms to cover scientific uncertainties, does not involve much of a challenge.

Thus, Clement identifies two ways of avoiding scientific errors that are legitimate only as minor elements in the kind of science fiction writing he espouses. The other strategies lead to the two forms commonly identified as hard science fiction.

The third way to avoid scientific errors is to play it safe: Set the story in the near future, and feature only scientific advances that are either already planned or completely plausible in light of current scientific and technological knowledge. Such stories, which almost always take place in outer space, have always been accepted as hard science fiction: one of the first works ever associated with the term was, as noted, Clarke's *A Fall of Moondust*, and all writers later identified with hard science fiction have occasionally written in this vein, such as Hal Clement's "Fireproof," Clarke's *Prelude to Space* and *Islands in the Sky*, Poul Anderson's "Sunjammer," and Larry Niven's "The Coldest Place." One could call this *microcosmic hard science fiction*—involving small steps into the future to predict small advances. In his own similar classification of the two types of hard science fiction, writer David Brin calls the form "engineering SF," which might discuss "a neat way in which the space shuttle might be used to rescue a doomed cosmonaut" or "how to pull off a successful revolt in a space colony with a 98 percent independent recycling system" ("Running Out of Speculative Niches" 9, 12-13).

Such stories are usually not seen as the most noteworthy examples of hard science fiction, and few would argue for the superiority of the listed works over Clement's *Mission of Gravity*, Clarke's *Rendezvous with Rama*, Anderson's *Tau Zero*, or Niven's *Ringworld*. Still, since many writers recognized as hard science fiction writers have produced works of this type, and since many such works have been called hard science fiction, I would argue that they must be accepted as part of the subgenre.

The fourth way to avoid scientific errors is a deliberate effort to create the most spectacular and implausible environment or development possible while at the same time adhering to all known scientific facts. One could call this "worldbuilding" *macrocosmic hard science fiction*—involving large leaps into the future to envision large advances and new worlds. Brin's term for this type is "scientific SF," where the writer "says 'What if?' in a grand way," dealing with questions like "the grand topic of life on the surface of a neutron star" or "the cosmological implications of Black Holes" ("Running Out of Speculative Niches" 9, 12-13).[3]

To most people, this is the most interesting form of hard science fiction, and it can certainly produce impressive results, like Clement's Mesklin and Larry Niven's *Ringworld*. But in terms of Clement's game, it is also a high-risk strategy: For example, after *Ringworld* was published, knowledgeable readers quickly pointed out that a structure like Ringworld could not maintain its position, which required Niven to awkwardly add stabilizing rockets in the sequel *Ringworld Engineers*; and another minor scientific problem with Ringworld was reported by Niven himself: "A Florida high-school class determined that all of the Ringworld's topsoil will end up in the oceans in a few thousand years" (introduction to an excerpt from *Ringworld* 123). In Clement's case, he also made a significant error in constructing Mesklin; as he later told Donald M. Hassler in an interview, "I was a little unhappy when the MIT science fiction people buckled down and analyzed Mesklin and found that I was wrong, that it would actually have come to a sharp edge at the equator" (cited in Hassler, *Hal Clement* 21).

"Whirligig World" is the first description of the process of writing this type of hard science fiction: Writers begin by accumulating and absorbing all available scientific information—in this case, information regarding the unseen companion to 61 Cygni; and, based on those data, writers carefully develop a detailed picture of the imagined environment, using equations when that is possible, informed guesswork when that is not possible. This process, ideally, should be as thoroughgoing as possible; Poul Anderson has remarked, "I've found that there is no such thing as too much background information when constructing an imaginary [planetary] system" ("Geology, Meteorology, Oceanography, Geography, Nomenclature, Biology" 25). Clement announces that "Whirligig World" is not designed as a "text" on how to create such worlds—"[I]f the subject is teachable I'd be creating competition and if it isn't I'd be wasting time" (102)— but actual texts later appeared, like Poul Anderson's "The Creation of Imaginary Worlds: The World Builder's Handbook and Pocket Companion" and Clement's own "The Creation of Imaginary Beings."

"Whirligig World" is also striking not because of what it discusses—the careful creation of a strange but scientifically possible world—but because of what it does not discuss—namely, how and why Clement developed a story to take place on that world. Clement does not explain why the Mesklinites were presented as businesslike traders or why the novel involved humans recruiting them to retrieve a fallen space probe. In "The Creation of Imaginary Beings," Clement explained the relationship between worldbuilding and storybuilding:

[T]here would seem to be two basic lines of procedure for the storyteller who needs nonhuman characters and other extraterrestrial life forms .... In the first case, the qualities of the various life forms have to a considerable extent already been determined ... by the story events .... [In] the second line, which is my favored technique .... I get most of the fun out of working out the physical and chemical nature of a planet or solar system, and then dreaming up life forms which might reasonably evolve under such conditions. The story (obviously, as some critics have been known to remark) comes afterward. (260-262)

In other words, the process of worldbuilding, in some cases, is undertaken to support a particular story, and, in other cases, is undertaken for its own sake, with a story tacked on later.

In a later interview, Clement specified in some detail exactly how he generated a story out of his worldbuilding:

When I have the planet pretty well worked out I think of as many non-standard things as I can think up that would happen on it, in what ways it would be different from Earth. Generally, I write these things down on index cards, and when the pile of cards is high enough I begin laying them out on the floor or on a card table or something, and I try to put them into some sort of chronological sensible order, and eventually I have a story. (Interview with Darrell Schweitzer 45)

As interviewer Darrell Schweitzer notes, the process "seems rather cut and dry" (45)—as if the story was being developed solely as a way to display the scientific and speculative detail.

Years later, in a related argument, Forward argues that the scientific background one develops effectively "writes the fiction." As examples, he notes that the astronomical setting he necessarily provided for the dwarf star in *Dragon's Egg* inspired details about his aliens' religious beliefs, and the strange characteristics of the magnetic field near its equator led to a key plot development ("When Science Writes the Fiction" 1-7). Anderson also claims that "the details are interesting in their own right .... many of them will suggest important parts of the plot" ("The Creation of Imaginary Worlds" 236-237). Niven and Jerry Pournelle agree that in hard science fiction, "Once the mechanical work is done the world may suggest a story, or it may even design its own inhabitants" ("Building The Mote in God's Eye" 347). Forward, Anderson, Niven, and Pournelle thus offer a third model for the relationship between background and story: The process of worldbuilding not only motivates the story, but actually creates the story.

These authors' explanations, however, seem disingenuous. First, despite attempts to minimize the notion of a preconceived story, all of them had at least a vague conception of their stories before they built their worlds. After all, why did Clement make Mesklin whirl so rapidly as to reduce its effective surface gravity in places to 3 Gs? Obviously—as implied by his statement that its originally calculated surface gravity was "over three hundred times what we're used to" ("Whirligig World" 106)—Clement wanted a world that humans could land on and survive on. Why did he provide Mesklin with oceans of liquid methane? Obviously—Clement said, "I want a native life form" ("Whirligig World" 110)—he wanted a world with indigenous intelligent life. It follows, then, that while the particulars of *Mission of Gravity*'s plot may well have developed at a later date, Clement from the beginning was attempting to create a world where visiting humans could contact native aliens. Forward is forthright about how the demands of his proposed story influenced how he made his world: "I knew I wanted the action to take place on a neutron star, and I knew that I wanted humans in the story, at least as bystanders" ("When Science Writes the Fiction" 4); explaining how he created the imaginary world Cleopatra, Poul Anderson says, "[W]e want to give [the star] a planet habitable to man" ("The Creation of Imaginary Worlds" 241); and describing the creation of *The Integral Trees*, Niven tells a similar story: "I had already decided to maroon a handful of human beings in the Smoke Ring, leave them alone for five hundred years, then see what they were up to. I needed oxygen, and therefore green plants. I needed normal sunlight, so I made the neutron star (Levoy's Star, or Voy) part of a binary. That implied oxygen; oxygen implied green plants" ("Blowing Smoke" 456-57). Thus, while the process of worldbuilding is undoubtedly constrained and shaped by scientific principles, it is also constrained to some extent by the demands of storytelling, whether the imagined story is vague or already detailed.

Still, Forward and Niven do have a point: It is often noted that scientific experimenters must be ready to notice unexpected as well as expected results;[4] similarly, the hard science fiction writer, during the process of worldbuilding, must be ready to explore unexpected as well as expected consequences of his scientific construct. As Forward said in advising hard science fiction writers, "[I]f the scientific facts are leading you away from your preconceived story line, don't hesitate to follow the lead" ("When Science Writes the Fiction" 4).

Reading about two forms of hard science fiction, some may argue that instead of establishing its two forms, I am defining two extremes of a hard science fiction continuum, with *Prelude to Space* at the near end and *Ringworld* at the far end. The concept is good in theory but is not realized in practice; that is, almost all of the works associated with hard science fiction tend to fall unambiguously into one of the two categories. Consider Clarke's novels. Works of microcosmic hard science fiction are clearly *Prelude to Space, Islands in the Sky, Sands of Mars, Earthlight, A Fall of Moondust, Dolphin Island, Imperial Earth, The Fountains of Paradise, The Ghost from the Grand Banks,* and *The Hammer of God.* Works of macrocosmic hard science fiction are clearly *Against the Fall of Night, Childhood's End, The City and the Stars, Rendezvous with Rama,* and *The Songs of Distant Earth.* The three *2001* novels each juxtapose—without blending—the two types, devoting most of their energy to a near-future space adventure with a stunning cosmic vision at the end—as is also seen in the brief far-future codas to *The Fountains of Paradise* and *The Ghost from the Grand Banks*. Other hard science fiction writers similarly begin in the near-future mode, then lurch forward into more extravagant environments: Forward's *The Flight of the Dragonfly* begins with a meticulous description of the construction of a laser-powered starship, then employs that ship to reach and explore a bizarre alien planet, Rocheworld. Charles Sheffield's *Between the Strokes of Night*, following a similar pattern, begins by discussing experiments in a near-future space station and steadily moves onward to an expansive adventure of galactic space exploration and revelation. Further, as will emerge from later discussions of representative texts, the differences between microcosmic and macrocosmic hard science fiction involve more than a change a scale; rather, there are also noteworthy shifts in generic model and overall tone.

Understanding the two forms of hard science fiction provides an answer to a recurring puzzle: apparent inconsistencies in the use of the term. This has become one of Norman Spinrad's favorite themes. For example, in his essay "Rubber Sciences," after defining the subgenre as "science fiction written around known scientific facts" (54), he makes these observations: even when the devices and backgrounds of Larry Niven, Hal Clement, and Poul Anderson are scientifically absurd, their work is unhesitatingly accepted as hard science fiction, but even when the devices and backgrounds of J. G. Ballard, Cordwainer Smith, and Mack Reynolds are scientifically logical, their work is not accepted as hard science fiction (54-55). The clear implication is that the term is being applied to certain writers in an arbitrary and illogical manner.[5]

Part of the answer to Spinrad's complaint no doubt lies in what could be called the sociology of the field. That is, authors identify themselves as hard science fiction writers by loudly announcing that fact, by publishing in magazines and anthologies like *Analog Science Fiction/Science Fact* and Jim Baen's *New Destinies* that have a reputation for hard science fiction, and by associating themselves with other well-known hard science fiction writers; authors who do not bother to do these things escape the label. Spinrad alludes to this process when he calls Gregory Benford "by far the most complete and literarily sophisticated novelist ever to have declared himself a hard science fiction writer" ("The Hard Stuff" 104); presumably, Spinrad suggests, Benford is regarded as a hard science fiction writer primarily because he regularly describes himself as one. And certainly, there have been other authors like Niven, Forward, and Brin who have no doubt earned the label of hard science fiction writers by repeatedly and vociferously calling themselves hard science fiction writers. However, since Clarke and others have been embraced by the subgenre without making any real efforts of this kind, there must be another explanation for patterns in the use of the label.

Noting that the focus of attention in early uses of the term involved what I call microcosmic hard science fiction, I offer this explanation (without defending it): Writing microcosmic hard science fiction defines a writer as a hard science fiction writer. More extravagant works are accepted as part of the form, but one demonstrates membership in the tribe by writing realistic, near-future space adventures, or by including such projections as part of more extravagant stories of constructed worlds. That is, Clarke is accepted as a hard science fiction writer because he can write stories like *A Fall of Moondust*, not just stories like *Childhood's End*; Clement because he can write stories like "Fireproof," not just stories like *Mission of Gravity*; Anderson because he can write stories like "Sunjammer," not just stories like *Tau Zero*; and so on. On the other hand, if writers do not bother to write stories of this kind, or apparently cannot write such stories, they will not be accepted as hard science fiction writers. That would explain why J. G. Ballard, Cordwainer Smith, and Mack Reynolds are rarely associated with the form.[6] And this attitude—based on an admittedly incomplete knowledge of recent commentaries—seems to survive to the present. Thus, recent writers like Benford, Forward, Brin, Sheffield, and James P. Hogan have each written examples of both forms of hard science fiction and hence are labelled as hard science fiction authors; but Ian Watson, who can be every bit as careful with his science as those writers, has generally not been so labeled, because he has not produced stories of microcosmic hard science fiction. The lesson for writers, then, is that if you wish to be considered a hard science fiction writer, building worlds may not be enough; it will also be helpful to demonstrate that you can build spaceships.[7]

What unites these two, apparently disparate forms of hard science fiction is an obsessive concern with complete accuracy and thorough development of all ideas—and this suggests one additional point: Contrary to some recent trends, not all science fiction stories that significantly involve science have been accepted as hard science fiction. Consider Fred Hoyle. As a prominent astronomer who regularly makes use of his knowledge in writing novels, Hoyle would apparently be an obvious example of the hard science fiction writer; as John Clute and Peter Nicholls observed, he "has brought a fine scientific mind to the background of his tales, strengthening them very considerably, and often giving readers an accurate sense of what it means to think like a scientist" ("Fred Hoyle" 295). This certainly sounds like the approach of a hard science fiction writer; yet Hoyle is usually not identified as such—even in Clute and Nicholls's article—and as noted, Miller's one reference to him employed the term *hard science story*, not *hard science fiction*, and was carefully conditional: his novel was "to a degree a 'hard'-type story."[8] Why, one asks, has Hoyle largely avoided the label of hard science fiction writer?

One answer comes in the "Preface" to Fred Hoyle and Geoffrey Hoyle's *Fifth Planet*, where they begin by announcing, "The very nature of the plot has forced us to set this story in the more distant future than we would otherwise have preferred. It is hardly possible to foresee the shape of society a century or more ahead of one's own time, and we have not attempted to do so" (v). Despite his attentiveness to the scientific accuracy of his central idea, then, Hoyle lacks the compulsion to comprehensively develop all aspects of his story; so if a story does not completely work out its scientific concepts or if it intermingles its scientific concepts with large doses of gobbledygook and fuzzy science, it will not truly qualify as hard science fiction—at best, it might be termed semihard science fiction.

It could also be argued that Hoyle's novels, like his steady state theory of the universe, often begin with an incredible assumption that is completely unconnected to current scientific knowledge—the sentient space cloud in *The Black Cloud*, the beings created by machines based on instructions broadcast from another galaxy in *A for Andromeda* and *Andromeda Breakthrough* (John Brosnan spoke of the original television series' "absurdities" ["*A for Andromeda*" 19]), and the regions from different time periods juxtaposed in *October the First Is Too Late*. True, once these premises are accepted, Hoyle develops them in a perfectly logical and scientific manner; but the technique of hard science fiction, as discussed by Clement and Forward, typically begins by building on the facts at hand, not on amazing assumptions. This could also explain why Hoyle is not regularly regarded as a practitioner of the form.

Adding together, then, what commentators like Miller, Blish and Ellison, and practitioners like Clement, Forward, and Brin, have had to say about hard science fiction, the following picture emerges: first, hard science fiction is a subgenre obsessed with total scientific accuracy. Practitioners sometimes acknowledge that complete scientific accuracy may be impossible—after all, Benford said, "There are no cheat-free stories, including my own" (cited in Huntington, "Hard-Core Science Fiction and the Illusion of Science" 50)—but such scientific accuracy is universally accepted as a *goal* in hard science fiction, though the extent to which it is always realized is another matter. Second, hard science fiction characteristically takes two forms—near-future space adventures and extravagant worldbuilding—and to be accepted as a hard science fiction writer, one must write hard science fiction of the first type, and one must be completely thorough, not selective, in scientific development in stories. Overall, noting that writers with scientific concerns who do not fulfill these criteria have usually not been accepted as hard science fiction writers, there is more logic and consistency in the typical use of the term than critics have noticed.

Much of what these writes say in discussing their own subgenre is similar to the statements of other commentators; however, there are significant differences. First, writers make little, if any, mention of the presence of long scientific explanations in their stories; perhaps they do not see such passages as necessary, or as important.[9] Also, writers repeatedly emphasize their activity as something playful, like a game, whereas commentators do not seem to sense such a spirit in the hard science fiction they read. Finally, more so than outsiders, the actual writers of hard science fiction are very cognizant of the expectations of their audience and build those expectations into their definitions of the subgenre. Consider, for example, the definition that Hal Clement once offered:

"Hard" science fiction is a recognizable field within a field; it is enjoyed largely by people who take their own scientific knowledge seriously; writing it therefore demands on the part of the author a fair amount of scientific knowledge and ability (partially replaceable by good research facilities and informed friends whose brains can be picked); and the worst mistake a hard science fiction writer can make, aside from failing to tell an entertaining story, is to write something that makes him look ignorant. He can disagree with accepted science, but he'd better have an impressive-sounding excuse. ("Hard Sciences and Tough Technologies" 51)

Thus, Clement adds a description of the characteristic *audience* of science fiction, an issue others may fail to discuss, and the idea that maintaining scientific accuracy is not relevant to some larger purposes but is more a matter of an author saving face—a point also made by Niven: "[Y]ou can't make up your own laws of physics. That's the surest way to get laughed out of the field" (Interview with Jeffrey M. Elliot, *Science Fiction Voices #2* 12).

Finally, there is one other quality of hard science fiction unrelated to scientific issues that is oddly, and repeatedly, mentioned by writers, almost as a defining characteristic: the absence of traditional literary values. Some hard science fiction writers openly criticize their own or others' abilities in this area. As already seen, Clement makes self-deprecating references to his own clumsiness in storytelling; he informed Donald M. Hassler that he was "not a literary writer" (*Hal Clement* 9); and he admitted to Darrell Schweitzer that "I don't consider that I'm very good at" characterization (Interview with Darrell Schweitzer 46). On a panel at the Eleventh Eaton Conference on Science Fiction and Fantasy, Forward flatly announced, "I have no writing style"; and Benford has spoken of Hoyle's "sometimes stiff characters and clumsy prose" and "the wordiness and melo-drama" of Tom Godwin's "The Cold Equations" ("Is There a Technological Fix for the Human Condition?" 84, 85). Furthermore, some commentators have accepted these shortcomings as true characteristics of the form. Thomas M. Disch included in his definition of *hard-core SF* the absence of "irony, aesthetic novelty," and "a tone of voice suggesting mature thoughtfulness" ("The Embarrassments of Science Fiction" 143); and Hassler announced that hard science fiction "is a growing body of literature that does not claim to be serious literature" (*Hal Clement* 7).

However, rather than proudly proclaiming this trait, some hard science fiction writers have lamented this general perception of poor writing in their subgenre. Benford describes "the conventional wisdom that, in hard SF, things were more important than people, intellect dominates over the heart, and that ideas, rather than experience, will play the leading role in setting, character and plot," though he argues that view is "fading" ("Is There a Technological Fix for the Human Condition?" 94), and Sheffield notes that "the hard SF label carries with it the stigma, or at least the suspicion, of poor characterization, tin ears, and a lack of sensitivity to everything that cannot be assigned a number" (Letter 4). Still, since these modern writers feel obliged to protest against this "conventional wisdom" or "stigma," it must remain widespread.

As a final conclusion to draw from this point, if a certain lack of literary polish is indeed regarded as one typical aspect of the form, then there may be another reason why writers like J. G. Ballard and Ian Watson have largely escaped the designation: namely, that they are excellent prose stylists.

Having shown that the term *hard science fiction* emerged in the late 1950s and early 1960s, that it was most frequently associated with writers of the 1950s and 1960s, and that the term has been associated with certain definable qualities, the question that can now be explored is: Exactly when did this kind of writing emerge? Does hard science fiction in fact have a long and distinguished history, or is it actually a relatively recent development?

NOTES

1. And gobbledygook remains the favored approach of some writers with no particular interest in or commitment to science; in lambasting the television movie *The Love War*, for example, Harlan Ellison did not complain about its egregious scientific errors but about the absence of jargon to cover those errors:

> Lloyd Bridges ... tries to explain ... the cosmography of Earth/Argon/Zinan ... he says they "overlap Earth" and that both planets are trying to take it over. Now, I am by no means Fred Hoyle or even Camille Flammarion, but I am several steps beyond a Cro-Magnon ... I can look up into the night sky and see that there are *not* two planets "overlapping" the Earth. Now, had the scenarists read even one 1930s issue of *Astounding Science Fiction*, they might have come up with the dodgem explanation that Argon (!) and Zinan "overlapped the Earth in another plane of existence" or used subspace, or another dimension .... one of a hundred writer's tricks sf authors have dreamed up ... to take care of such problems. ("20 March 70" 40)

2. Indeed, the initial focus of hard science fiction on engineering and hard sciences may only reflect the fact that in the 1950s not enough was known about life processes to construct aliens in convincing detail. Twenty years later, that was no longer the case, so Clement himself was able to write an article on "The Creation of Imaginary Beings" in 1974. One also finds recent stories, like Michael E. Flynn's "The Washer at the Ford" that follow the classic hard science fiction pattern but focus on biological, not mechanical, engineering—in Flynn's case, a bioengineered "nanny" that

could repair the effects of radiation poisoning. However, Gregory Benford has argued that there is in fact a special affinity between hard science and hard science fiction: "While botany, or human anatomy, or zoology do not really separate us from our common world, physics, chemistry, and especially astronomy certainly do. This alienation may be why these latter sciences turn up so much in hard sf, as it struggles with the emotions they kindle" ("Real Science, Imaginary Worlds" 16).

3. While Brin provides the best support for the notion of these two forms of hard science fiction, there is a glimmering of the categories in P. Schuyler Miller's distinctions between the "documentary" and "poetic" Clarke, and Algis Budrys's distinction between the "mystical" and the "hard" Clarke. Also worth noting is that Benford once casually defined "the 'hard' kind of science fiction" as "namely, rocket ships, strange planets, etc."—suggesting microcosmic hard science fiction with "rocket ships" and macrocosmic hard science fiction with "strange planets" (Interview with Jeffrey M. Elliot 47).

4. A famous example of a scientist noticing important, though unanticipated, experimental results is discussed in Lewis Thomas's *The Youngest Science* (155-158).

5. Spinrad repeats the argument in "The Hard Stuff" (94-95) and concludes that differences between hard science fiction and other science fiction do not involve scientific rigor but the center of attention. That is, Harry Harrison's *West of Eden* and *Winter in Eden* are hard science fiction because the focus is Harrison's scientific ideas, but Ballard's novels are not part of the subgenre because he "uses the hard science content primarily to set up an altered psychic landscape and emphasizes the general literary concerns over the scientific speculation" (99).

6. After Spinrad's 1976 essay, Reynolds did write some novels about near-future space habitats—*Lagrange Five*, *Chaos in Lagrangia*, and *Trojan Orbit* (the latter with Dean Ing)—which should have admitted him to the subgenre. Perhaps Reynolds converted to the form too late to change popular perceptions—just as Clifford D. Simak, after forty years of writing science fiction, was never accepted as a fantasy writer, despite several later novels in that genre.

7. While writing only macrocosmic hard science fiction excludes one from the ranks of hard science fiction writers, there is a corresponding but weaker phenomenon: Writing only microcosmic hard science fiction tends to define one as a peripheral writer. Consider Ben Bova. With his scientific background and stories focused on technology, Bova might seem a quintessential hard science fiction writer; yet he is rarely mentioned in discussions of hard science fiction. The problem may be that he specializes in cautious near-future predictions and rarely engages in more expansive worldbuilding. To be a hard science fiction writer of the first rank, it seems, one must build both spaceships and worlds.

8. Gregory Benford, usually a bit more expansive about such matters, unambiguously embraces Hoyle as a hard science fiction writer ("Is There a Technological Fix for the Human Condition?" 84, 94); "Real Science, Imaginary Worlds" 19).

9. However, Benford did note that in hard science fiction, "[t]he drone of meticulous explanation appears often, almost like a bizarre fetish" ("Real Science, Imaginary Worlds" 18).

5

"The Best 'Hard' Science Fiction of Its Day": An Inquiry into the Origins of Hard Science Fiction

As already discussed, the concept of hard science fiction, and the term, originated in the 1950s and 1960s, and the label has been most frequently employed to describe writers of those eras. This would seem to suggest that hard science fiction itself also emerged during these times. However, I have also noted sporadic and partial efforts in the 1930s and 1940s to define a form of hard science fiction, which might suggest an earlier origin date. More significantly, one also finds in modern documents repeated assertions that hard science fiction is a much older form. A minor theme is that a few prominent writers who preceded or wrote outside of the genre of science fiction—like Nathaniel Hawthorne, Edgar Allan Poe, Jules Verne, Rudyard Kipling, H. G. Wells, and Olaf Stapledon—can be called hard science fiction writers; a major theme is that hard science fiction was in fact a dominant, if not *the* dominant, form of genre science fiction before 1950. Based on what I have traced as the critical history of hard science fiction, however, one must question if either characterizations is accurate.

While science fiction commentators have freely extended the history of science fiction back to Jonathan Swift, Thomas More, Lucian, Aristophanes, and Plato, hard science fiction commentators have generally been more restrained in finding ancient antecedents. Only twice to my knowledge has the term been applied to writers before the nineteenth century: in Paul Alkon's examination of Thomas Burnet ("Thomas Burnet's *Sacred Theory of the Earth* and the Aesthetics of Extrapolation") in the critical anthology *Hard Science Fiction*, and in Sam Moskowitz's comment that Daniel Defoe's *Robinson Crusoe* and the anonymous *The History of Automathes* were "the hard science fiction of the period" ("The Origins of Science Fiction Fandom" 12). And Hawthorne, Poe, and Kipling have been added to the field only by David G. Hartwell and Kathryn Cramer in their anthology *The Ascent of Wonder*.

However, there have been numerous efforts to establish Verne as a hard science fiction writer. As noted above, C. S. Lewis included *Twenty Thousand Leagues under the Sea* in his category "Engineers' Stories"; Miller's review stated that Lewis's term was equivalent to his "documentary approach," one of his loose synonyms for hard science fiction; and L. David Allen identified Verne as "the archetypal practitioner of Extrapolative Hard Science Fiction" (*Science Fiction* 13). More recently, Frank McConnell spoke of "[t]he hard Sf writer, from Verne to Asimov to Larry Niven" ("Sturgeon's Law" 17); Norman Spinrad, discussing hard science fiction, said, "Some trace its origins back to Jules Verne" ("The Hard Stuff" 93); in a 1987 column, Bruce Sterling said that "Jules Verne had invented hard science fiction. He originated the hard SF metier of off-the-rack plots and characters, combined with vast expository lumps of pop science," and he described Verne's criticism of Wells's Cavorite as "the most famous exemplar of the hard-SF writer's eternal plaint against the fantasist" ("Midnight on the Rue Jules Verne" 63, 64); and Verne scholar Arthur B. Evans has flatly declared that Verne was "*the* originator of 'hard' science fiction" (Letter to Gary Westfahl).

As for Wells and Stapledon, Wells was freely accepted as a hard science fiction writer by two early and noteworthy commentators, James Blish and John W. Campbell, Jr, and Stapledon has been called a hard science fiction writer by Gregory Benford ("Is There a Technological Fix for the Human Condition?") and McConnell, who, as noted, called *Star Maker* "the hardest of hard SF stories" ("Sturgeon's Law" 22). Similarly, in listing the debts of cyberpunk fiction to "the harder tradition" of science fiction, Bruce Sterling includes "the science/politics of H. G. Wells" and "the cosmic outlook of Olaf Stapledon," incorporating them as hard science fiction writers ("Preface" to *Mirrorshades* x). The rationale in all cases seems that these writers had some scientific knowledge and training and were serious in using and thinking about science in their imaginative creations.

Still, I feel there is one broad objection to make to all of these characterizations. Hal Clement has argued, and other hard science fiction writers have agreed, that hard science fiction writers develop and describe their worlds with a determination to avoid scientific errors and with an expectation that knowledgeable readers will be alert to notice and complain about any errors that do crop up. This is the game of hard science fiction. And such a context of shared concerns did not exist for Wells, Stapledon, and their contemporary readers. No one in these writers' milieu regarded absolute scientific accuracy as important; so Wells and Stapledon, lacking such an audience, had no incentive to worry too much about such accuracy.[1] Verne, one might argue, was an exceptional case. As Evans notes, "Verne himself was always very careful to verify his scientific facts with experts before putting them into his texts," and "a relatively large segment of his reading public were scientists and engineers who ... would have jumped all over him for any error or excessive extrapolation" (Letter to Gary Westfahl).

Perhaps Verne managed to create for himself a temporary context where the game of hard science fiction could be played; still, he apparently did not manage to create a strong and lasting tradition of writers and readers who maintained that context. He would be, then, not quite the originator of hard science fiction, but an "anticipator" of the subgenre.[2]

One can also argue that these writers were, in fact, not always accurate in their science—even Verne. With the physics of the time, one could determine that Verne's space gun in *From the Earth to the Moon* would crush its occupants; as already noted, Gernsback was obliged to apologize at length for the scientific idiocies in *Off on a Comet*; and John W. Campbell, Jr., once observed that Verne's "bright new dreams look rather silly now—his air machine in 'Robur the Conqueror' is, as every twelve-year-old now knows, aerodynamically impossible. Most of his wild inventions are old stuff, and he's got 'em all wrong" ("We Can't Keep Up!" 6). Wells was certainly enough of a biologist to know that it was highly unlikely the Martian creatures of *The War of the Worlds* would be affected by terrestrial germs; and Stapledon's *Last and First Men* and *Star Maker* include concepts—such as intelligent stars and Martian energy-beings—that are difficult to justify based on the scientific knowledge of his time. Perhaps the best thing to say about these writers would be to paraphrase Campbell's description of Wells and call them the hard science fiction writers *of their day*—writers who came as close to the ideals of hard science fiction as the circumstances of their careers allowed, but not completely fulfilling those ideals.

A more powerful argument, often observed in both laudatory and critical comments about hard science fiction, is that the subgenre represents an older and more traditional type of modern science fiction. As noted, the first two books P. Schuyler Miller labelled hard science fiction were Campbell's *Islands of Space* (originally published in 1931) and George O. Smith's *Venus Equilateral* (originally published in 1942-1945). In addition, Miller called James Blish's "'hard science' story" *The Triumph of Time* "almost an anachronism" (August 1959 151), said that Arthur C. Clarke's *A Fall of Moondust* "is the kind of book that proves that 'old-fashioned' science fiction isn't dead" (February 1962 164), spoke of "the 'hard' technical science fiction of a generation ago" (January 1963 170) and "of the early years" (May, 1964 89), and said that "The Permanent Implosion" and "Sunjammer" "will take you back to the 'Good Old Days'" of George O. Smith and Jack Williamson (December 1966 160-161). As noted, Poul Anderson began a 1961 response to Hal Clement by saying, "I am delighted that the Game is still being played," as if fearful that hard science fiction was already becoming a lost art ("Brass Tacks" 172). And in 1968, lambasting "[t]he Campbell heavy-science story" as represented by Frank Herbert's *The Dragon in the Sea*, Harlan Ellison declared, "What began as a New Wave in the Forties with Campbell's rejection of the Crustacean Period in speculative fiction .... has now come far past the end of its passage, and now represents something like a return to the T. O'Connor Sloane [*sic*] image of what a *good* science fiction story should be" ("A Voice from the Styx" 125, 122-123). Miller, Anderson, and Ellison thus seem to envision recent writers of hard science fiction like Clarke and Herbert as the lonely survivors of an earlier form of science fiction—a view echoed somewhat by Clement, who, as noted, called Anderson and Larry Niven "hard science fiction types, as close to the old style space opera as you can get" (Interview with Darrell Schweitzer 51). And Isaac Asimov would apparently agree with these characterizations, since he once said, "The 1940s and 1950s were the heyday of 'hard science fiction'" ("Science Fiction Today" 293).

Academic critics tend to accept this view. John Huntington's "Hard-Core Science Fiction and the Illusion of Science" confidently states, "By the nineteen fifties the genre of the hard core has been established" (49). George Slusser's "The Ideal Worlds of Science Fiction" asserts that Isaac Asimov was "once considered the father of hard SF" (233). As noted, Carol McGuirk saw hard science fiction as beginning "shortly before World War II" and lists as "honorary latecomers and converts" Larry Niven, George Zebrowski, and Gregory Benford ("The 'New' Romancers" 111). William Bainbridge's *Dimensions of Science Fiction* traces hard science fiction back even further—to the days of Hugo Gernsback's *Amazing Stories*, claiming "Gernsback's approach was what today we would call hard science" (54).

The strength of these arguments is that the ideas that drive hard science fiction —powerful concerns for scientific accuracy and logical scientific thinking—can easily be traced to early science fiction commentators, and thus might have actually had an influence on those early writers. Gernsback was certainly the first to repeatedly emphasize that science fiction must "contain correct scientific facts" ("$500.00 Prize Story Contest" 773) and must present those facts in clear language; and recognizing the importance of that principle, Lester del Rey begins discussing Clement's career by saying, "When Hugo Gernsback started the first science-fiction magazine back in 1926, he didn't refer to hard science fiction; but he did claim that his stories were scientifically accurate" ("Introduction" xi).

Readers quickly accepted Gernsback's idea, and they started to complain about stories that were not "scientifically accurate": one said, "[S]ome of the stories have such obvious scientific mistakes in them that they seem more like fairy tales" (cited in "Plausibility in Scientifiction" 675), while another reader urged Gernsback to only publish stories that featured factual information: "[B]e sure to have the science in the stories correct so that I shall not be obliged to put the ban on them" ("Discussions," February, 1927 1077).[3]

Since many of his readers seemed to enjoy finding errors in stories, Gernsback finally made a contest out of it. Publishing Geoffrey Hewelcke's "Ten Million Miles Sunward," he announced, "Frankly, though, there is something wrong with the story" and challenged readers, "See if you can find out what that 'something' is" (introduction to "Ten Million Miles Sunward" 1127). This contest could be said to anticipate the game that Clement and several other writers would later see at the heart of hard science fiction. In addition, one can find stories from this era that seem to fit into the parameters of microcosmic hard science fiction. Consider Gernsback's "The Magnetic Storm." This 1917 story is set in the near future, while World War I is still raging, and it involves a perfectly practical application of then-current technology—a large-scale effort to generate magnetic fields that will disable enemy equipment, endorsed as feasible by no less than Nicolas Tesla.[4] This was, by the way, exactly the type of story Gernsback had in mind when he proposed the category of *science faction*.

As for macrocosmic hard science fiction, the idea behind this type of writing—at least the process of writing it—can be traced back to the theories of Campbell, who declared that "Science-Fiction, being largely an attempt to forecast the future, on the basis of the present, represents a type of extrapolation" ("The Perfect Machine" 5), and "Mapping out a civilization of the future is an essential background to a convincing story of the future .... [Y]ou've got to have that carefully mapped outline in mind to get consistency of minor details" ("The Old Navy Game" 6). And by publishing Robert A. Heinlein's "Future History" chart in 1941, graphically displaying a carefully worked out background for many Heinlein stories, he seemed to offer an example of the process and its benefits. Another Campbell author, Isaac Asimov, with his Foundation and Robot stories, also appeared to represent the process of careful extrapolation and development of future societies.

However, I see a number of problems involved in seeing Gernsback, Campbell, and their writers as the true originators of hard science fiction. First, despite his announced theories, Gernsback, as noted, was willing to publish stories with dubious or fuzzy science and sometimes admitted as much. Campbell could also be inattentive to scientific errors; he published A. E. van Vogt's "Concealment" without bothering to correct its obvious blunder—a "meteorite station" in space.[5] The example of van Vogt also shows he was not particularly emphatic in demanding careful extrapolative thinking: as Damon Knight demonstrated, the Earth of *The World of Null-A* "would be a plausible, if sketchy, background for a story laid from 50 to 100 years in the future. For a story which takes place 600 years from now, it is as bad as no background at all .... van Vogt has not bothered to integrate the gadgets into the technological background of his story" (*In Search of Wonder* 55-56).

Despite the fact that the literature of this era later developed a reputation for focusing on science, then, there is some truth in the charge of Peter Nicholls and John Sladek: "Sf in the days of the pulp magazines was very much more prone to [scientific] error than it is now .... Most sf written in the 1960s and '70s will pass scientific muster with readers who have a little university-level science, but the excesses of the 1920s and '30s must have been obvious to readers who had only a smattering of high-school science" ("Scientific Errors" 532). Making a similar point, Paul Carter says, "This cautious, don't-get-caught-in-a-mistake mentality, so characteristic of the 1980s, is in striking contrast to the go-for-broke, cheerleading ethos of World War II" ("You Can Write Science Fiction If You Want To" 142).

Furthermore, in keeping with this tacit atmosphere of scientific laxity, few works of the 1930s and 1940s completely fulfill the criteria of hard science fiction. Gernsback may have liked plausible stories of *science faction* set in the near future, but his readers did not: they clamored for far-ranging "interplanetary stories." And, with the knowledge and technology then available, such adventures could not be written as *science faction*. Some writers tried: while presenting space station Gaudien, J. M. Walsh's *Vandals of the Void* (1930) claimed as a source Hermann von Noordung's *The Problems of Space Flying*: "The plans for the Gaudien were actually based on designs drawn up so long ago as the year 1929 by Captain Hermann Noordung, a German engineer and authority on mechanics, who was perhaps the first of all Earth-men to deal with the problem of space navigation seriously" (482). But the design of the station is actually not presented in all that much detail—necessarily, since it was envisioned as larger and more elaborate than von Noordung's station—and there is little, if any, scientific substance to the rest of Walsh's novel, a thoroughly routine space adventure.

The author before World War II who came the closest to writing microcosmic hard science fiction was undoubtedly George O. Smith, so that there is some justice in the fact that he was the second author to be given the label. That is, in the early series of stories later collected in *Venus Equilateral*, Smith attempted to address and intelligently resolve some of the problems involved in space communication (though he occasionally overcomplicated matters—one story, for instance, concerns the incredible difficulty of sending a radio message to a spaceship). His space station was thought out and presented with unusual care and thoroughness; and in describing the odd camaraderie that developed among its residents, Smith was attempting to develop his station into a detailed and convincing future environment. The problem was that there were only so many stories in this vein that Smith could write, so he was eventually driven into the realm of pseudoscience by having the scientists at Venus Equilateral design and perfect a method of matter transmissions, with various implausible results.

Another point about Smith: his works were commonly seen as *scientific problem stories*, the sporadically accepted subgenre of science fiction discussed above; and some of Miller's comments suggest that he saw these stories as hard science fiction: he called Simak's "Limiting Factor" both "a puzzle story" and "'hard' science fiction" (September 1962 155). Also, while not using the term, Sam Moskowitz's *Seekers of Tomorrow* is emphatic in arguing that hard science fiction is an outgrowth of this form, calling *Mission of Gravity* "what is generally regarded as the epic of the scientific problem story in science fiction," and describing Ross Rocklynne as the first "popularizer" of the subgenre (415-416).

However, with the exception of Smith, these authors cannot really be regarded as practitioners of the form. For one thing, like other science fiction writers of their time, they are sometimes prone to incredible scientific errors, Rocklynne's "At the Center of Gravity" being a prominent example; as readers immediately pointed out, a large hollow sphere in the story would attract objects to its surface, not to its center as Rocklynne indicated. Second, these writers are typically so focused on the problem at hand that they may neglect to explore the other important aspects of their imagined worlds. Asimov's comments on his "The Talking Stone" are revelatory: "After the story first appeared, I received quite a bit of mail expressing interest in the silicony [a silicon creature living in the asteroid belt] and, in some cases, finding fault with me for allowing it to die in so cold-blooded a fashion .... I must admit the readers are right. I showed a lack of sensitivity to the silicony's rather pathetic death because I was concentrating on his mysterious last words" ("Afterword" to "The Talking Stone" 53-54). Focused on presenting and resolving their mysteries, writers of scientific problem stories may not completely explore all the scientific implications in the materials developed for their stories—but Robert F. Forward would later define an open-minded, exploratory attitude as one attribute of the hard science fiction writer. Thus, while "The Talking Stone" is well grounded in science, Asimov fails—at least in this instance—to fulfil all the requirements of hard science fiction.

While Asimov's story is a relatively recent example, similar inattentiveness to interesting issues can also be seen in earlier *scientific problem stories*. In Rocklynne's "The Men and the Mirror," for example, his policeman Colbey and criminal Deverel stumble upon a gigantic, perfectly formed concave mirror on a planetary surface, constructed by some ancient alien culture; and Rocklynne offers a few words of speculation about what kind of civilization would construct such a mirror, and for what reason—questions worth exploring. But the matter is quickly dropped, as Colbey and Deverel's preoccupation becomes devising a method to stop sliding up and down the mirror's surface, and there is no further discussion of the artifact's creators or purpose.

Only after World War II, when the United States actually developed a space program, and when realistic and concrete proposals for spaceships, space stations, and space missions were widely promulgated, could outer space become a fit subject for *science faction*. In some respects, the breakthrough novel in this case was Arthur C. Clarke's *Prelude to Space*—originally written in 1947, although not published until 1951. As Clarke reported in his 1961 Foreword, "When writing this novel, I had the great advantage of access to calculations which my colleagues A. V. Cleaver and L. R. Shepherd were making on the subject of nuclear rocket propulsion. These were later published in their classic paper 'The Atomic Rocket' (*Journal of the British Interplanetary Society*, September 1948-

March 1949) which is still widely quoted in the field" (6). In addition to using up-to-date scientific materials, Clarke also strived to extrapolate exactly how successful flight to the Moon might actually occur. Thus, the novel has no eccentric inventor building a spaceship in his backyard but, rather, envisions a large, government-sponsored project to construct and launch a manned rocket; and while there is one episode involving an ineffectual saboteur, Clarke generally avoids the atmosphere of melodramatic adventure and instead presents space travel as a businesslike, though visionary, enterprise. Like other British writers, Clarke erred in seeing his own country as the inaugurator of space flight from a base in Australia, but in other respects, the book is a remarkably accurate anticipation of the actual space program. Other early Clarke novels similarly used published data to present realistic pictures of space stations in operation, as in *Islands in the Sky*; new and more accurate information about the moon produced *Earthlight* and *A Fall of Moondust*; and continuing observation of the planet Mars led to *Sands of Mars*, arguably the first Mars story built on an accurate scientific assessment of conditions on that planet.

The type of story represented by *Prelude to Space*—one set in the near future and featuring apparently realistic and predictable space technology employed to explore and inhabit the solar system—in fact became widespread in the 1950s: It constituted the dominant form of the new subgenre of juvenile science fiction, and more than enough stories of this type were written for the adult market. My own research in space stations in science fiction, for example, reveals that about 120 stories and novels about space stations were published between 1950 and 1959—almost all of them depictions of building and occupying space stations in Earth orbit in the near future.[6] In effect, when the exciting environment of space entered the realm of foreseeable and practical technology, microcosmic hard science fiction truly emerged.

Before 1950, there were also few, if any, examples of macrocosmic hard science fiction—spectacular worldbuilding following scientific principles. One must acknowledge Miller's early characterization of John W. Campbell, Jr.'s *Islands of Space* as "characteristic of the best 'hard' science fiction of its day" (November 1957 143)—but that qualifying phrase "of its day" cannot be ignored: for all of his detailed and apparently logical scientific explanations, Campbell was simply not engaged in building up anything like a thorough and logical future world in the manner that would later be defined as characteristic of hard science fiction. In a later letter to Hal Clement, Campbell effectively admitted that his own stories were not really examples of hard science fiction: "Precise, jig-saw-puzzle interlocking of details wasn't a forte of mine; the highly pleasing results you've produced by doing so has taught me that it's a satisfying thing to do, instead of being merely a damn nuisance" (Letter to Hal Clement 151).

Isaac Asimov and Robert A. Heinlein are surely better candidates for examples of early worldbuilders, but they were actually not all that attentive in developing the background universes of their Foundation and Future History series. Asimov has frequently admitted that he more or less made up the Foundation universe as he went along, and later novels like his *Robots and Empire* devote a considerable amount of energy to explaining and rationalizing aspects of that series that should have been resolved long ago. Heinlein was a bit more careful; and, as Smith represents the closest prewar approach to microcosmic hard science fiction, Heinlein undoubtedly represents the closest prewar approach to macrocosmic hard science fiction. And Heinlein undoubtedly was a major influence on later hard science fiction writers. When asked about his reputation as a "builder of civilizations" why he chose "the future history mode," Poul Anderson replied, "Of course, I was influenced by Robert Heinlein, who wrote an outstanding future history. As far as I know, the future history approach originated with him" (Interview with Jeffrey M. Elliot 47).

However, considered as a hard science fiction writer, Heinlein had his conspicuous lapses as well; for many years, he included the story "'We Also Walk Dogs—'" in his Future History even though it contradicted many details in other stories, and after introducing an orbiting power plant in "Blowups Happen," he failed to mention it in later stories, and only in his very last novel, *To Sail Beyond the Sunset*, did he get around to explaining its conspicuous absence in other works. The future environments offered by Asimov and Heinlein may also be perfunctory: their future cities in *The Caves of Steel* and *Beyond This Horizon* are impressive, but their alien worlds are nothing like Mesklin or Ringworld. Thus, neither writer fully anticipates the process and possibilities of hard science fiction that Clement and Niven later demonstrated—a conclusion echoed by Samuelson, who called the two writers, "Rarely typical of hard sf" ("A Softening of the Hard-Sf Concept" 412).

To explain the rise of macrocosmic hard science fiction in the 1950s, one might observe that at this time of significant developments in space technology there were also less dramatic, but equally impressive gains, in astronomical knowledge about other planets. *Mission of Gravity*, for example, is noteworthy not only as an impressive piece of planetbuilding, but as the first science fiction novel built on actual scientific research involving another possible solar system; as Clement reported in "Whirligig World," the "basic idea" for the novel derived from the work of a scientist who, in 1943, "published the results of some incredibly—to anyone but an astronomer—painstaking work on the orbit of the binary star 61 Cygni .... [H]e was not only able to publish a more accurate set of orbital elements than had previously been available, but to show that the orbital motion was not regular .... One of the two stars ... was actually accompanied by another, invisible object" (104). And Clement built Mesklin based on the parameters established by that research, just as Clarke constructed his moon rocket based on the work of Cleaver and Shepherd. Thus, what is unquestionably the breakthrough novel of macrocosmic hard science fiction emerged directly from new astronomical discoveries.

Overall, the work of Clarke and Clement in the early 1950s shows an attentiveness to recent scientific research and thoughtful scientific extrapolation that is simply not present in most works of earlier eras. Thus, another one of Miller's comments seems the best description of the role of science in science fiction before 1950: Speaking of an anthology of Russian science fiction, he said, "As we did a generation ago, the writers here rely on hyperbole—on writing in a sustained shout—rather than on 'hard' science" (October 1968 162).

Indeed, "hyperbole" and "a sustained shout" are, overall, an excellent description of most science fiction before 1950—which brings up another common misconception: namely, that *Astounding Science-Fiction* and writers like Asimov and Heinlein were representative of science fiction in the 1940s. This is a patently false picture that emerges from a close study of *The Science Fiction Hall of Fame*, not a close study of the actual publications of the period. First, even within the hallowed pages of *Astounding*, Campbell was publishing any number of writers—including E. E. "Doc" Smith, A. E. van Vogt, and A. Bertram Chandler—whose work could by no stretch of the imagination be described as *hard science fiction*. Second, the other magazines of the period, including *Amazing Stories, Thrilling Wonder Stories*, and *Planet Stories*, all conspicuously failed to place much emphasis on scientific accuracy and thinking.[7] Therefore, even if a critic were to grant George O. Smith, Asimov, and Heinlein the status of true hard science fiction writers, she would be hard- pressed to locate more good candidates from that period of science fiction history.

It seems best, then, to see hard science fiction as a development of the 1950s and 1960s, when writers emerged who were determined to practice what Gernsback and Campbell had preached, who had access to new data and detailed plans, and who elevated scientific accuracy and extrapolative thinking to the central positions in the writing of science fiction they had previously enjoyed only in theory. This seems close to Samuelson's position, given his comment, "Since by any account hard sf is a recent conception, Poe, Hawthorne, and Miles J. Breuer, M.D. [in *The Ascent of Wonder*] are also anachronisms" ("A Softening of the Hard-Sf Concept" 410). This suggests a fundamental shift in the ways the modern history of science fiction is characterized.

The conventional picture is that the literature of the 1930s and 1940s was dominated by science and technology; then, in the 1950s and 1960s, writers began to shift away from a focus on science to other, nonscientific priorities; thus, after identifying the 1940s as the period when hard science fiction emerged, Carol McGuirk speaks of "the subsequent soft science fiction movement that dominated the field throughout the 1950s." This trend culminated in the New Wave movement of the 1960s: McGuirk says the New Wave sought to "widen [science fiction's] intertextual and allusive base beyond even the wide boundaries set by early soft science fiction" and that "the first generation of soft science fiction writers lost the center stage, and a younger, more aggressive generation of soft stylists seized it"; her conclusion is that "the new wave developed organically from the soft SF of the 1950s rather than representing ... a sudden break" ("The 'New' Romancers" 115, 121, 122). Then, as a violent reaction to the excesses of the New Wave, a counterrevolution in favor of older, more scientific science fiction was launched in the name of *hard science fiction*.

I am now prepared to venture a different hypothesis: namely, that despite public pronouncements, science fiction was in fact largely indifferent to science before 1950 and conspicuously tolerated frequent errors and inattentiveness to scientific fact and scientific thinking. Only after 1950 did a school of writers emerge who transformed previously announced scientific priorities into firm rules of science fiction and developed two specific forms of science fiction that responded to those rules. The result was an explosion of scientifically-oriented stories in the 1950s and 1960s, largely unnoticed by literary critics because it involved texts and authors they were not overly concerned with—such as juvenile science fiction and the lesser *Astounding/Analog* writers. Therefore, considered by weight of numbers alone, it may be that hard science fiction, not soft science fiction, actually "dominated the field throughout the 1950s."

By the early 1960s, it might have seemed to some observers that this form of writing was in fact starting to become the major force in the genre. A number of new writers practicing and preaching a science-oriented style had appeared and were increasing in prominence; most of the minor magazines that had been open to a wide variety of science fiction had vanished; *Astounding Science-Fiction* became *Analog: Science Fact/Science Fiction* (later, *Analog Science Fiction/Science Fact*) and vigorously established a greater emphasis on science and technology; *Galaxy* and *If* were now edited by Frederik Pohl, who was more concerned about science than predecessor H. L. Gold; even *The Magazine of Fantasy and Science Fiction* seemed to shift to a greater emphasis on science under Robert P. Mills, with its science articles by Asimov, among other things. And in the context of an apparent shift to more science in science fiction, the New Wave—at least its American version—may have been a counterrevolution, an effort to shift the genre back to its previous laxity regarding scientific matters.

As one piece of evidence for this hypothesis, consider Harlan Ellison's assault on Herbert's *The Dragon in the Sea*. Amidst much criticism of the novel's style and characterization, Ellison lambastes its emphasis on scientific discussions:

[T]he sole reason for the existence of this novel is the gleeful and meticulous explication of the minutiae of hardware aboard the *Fenian Ram*. This is a gear-and-grommet story. It is an engineer's daydream .... not a novel, nor a study of people, nor an attempt to point a moral, or tell a story, or entertain a reader; it is shop talk .... More and more, Campbell has leaned toward writers who are not writers; engineers and scientists who have been able to transpose theories and mechanical developments in their certain fields into shallow stories, mere vehicles for the science

.... *Analog* has not even been in the running [for the Best Magazine Hugo Award] for half a dozen years. This ... seems highly unusual, until one considers that those copies are being sold to the other members of the bull session—other engineers and scientists.

Clearly, Ellison finds the conversations of science fiction he once enjoyed increasingly dominated by "engineers and scientists" and "shop talk" which he is not interested in and cannot participate in; and his call for "a new definition ... of the form" is an effort to shift the conversation back to a style and subject matter he is more comfortable with ("A Voice from the Styx" 121, 124, 123).

Further evidence for this hypothesis would demand thorough statistical analysis; but Anderson's 1973 essay "The Science" provides some suggestive data. Using his own idiosyncratic classification system of "hard science," "imaginary science," "quasiscience," and "counter-science," Anderson surveyed and classified the novels and stories that were either nominated for or won Nebula Awards, and he concluded that "hard science and technophilia are flourishing—maybe more than ever!" Another survey of winners of Hugo Awards and the International Fantasy Awards produced a similar result: "Evidently readers continue to go for 'traditional' sf" ("The Science" 272, 273). And that survey only included noteworthy works that were nominated for or won awards; a tabulation of run-of-the-mill stories from the 1960s might possibly show an even greater preponderance of highly scientific works. (Certainly almost all of the stories published in *Analog* during that period, for example, would qualify.)

Although the form and concept of hard science fiction, then, was already well established by the time the New Wave appeared, it is undoubtedly true that the prominent excesses of the New Wave engendered a countervailing spirit of advocacy among practitioners and fans of hard science fiction; and Larry Niven, as the one major new writer of the 1960s who specialized in hard science fiction, was one rallying point for such advocates: Gregory Benford, for example, has said that "Larry was a breath of Campbellian clarity in the New Wave murk" ("On Niven" 4). In addition, the New Wave probably contributed to the trend in the 1970s, already noted, to employ the term hard science fiction essentially to designate all types of science fiction that were emphatically not part of the New Wave. Thus, while the term *hard science fiction* became common in the 1960s, it was certainly the 1970s that brought it to the forefront. My point is that writers like Niven, Benford, Pournelle, Hogan, Sheffield, and Forward do not represent a new outburst of interest in science but rather represent a continuation of a commitment to hard science fiction that began earlier, in the 1950s and 1960s.

One other point: Understanding that the concept of hard science fiction emerged before and during the period of the New Wave, not afterward, may explain the common modern tendency to divide all science fiction into *hard science fiction* and *soft science fiction*, while also acknowledging the presence of a third category of *fantasy* associated with but not necessarily part of the genre. Thus, L. David Allen's *Science Fiction: An Introduction* divides science fiction into hard science fiction, soft science fiction, science-fantasy, and fantasy; William Bainbridge's *Dimensions of Science Fiction* establishes three basic categories of science fiction as hard science, New Wave, and fantasy; and George Slusser's "The Ideal Worlds of Science Fiction" speaks of science fiction being divided into three groups—hard science fiction, soft science fiction, and horror.

The origin of this viewpoint is illuminated by considering the data that Bainbridge employed to build his mapping of science fiction—a survey of science fiction fans, conducted in 1979, whose average date of birth was 1951 or 1952 (*Dimensions of Science Fiction* 21). Since I was born in 1951, I can speak with personal authority about how persons of that age would come to perceive of science fiction. Like many others, I began reading science fiction regularly at the age of ten; and as a teenager in the 1960s, science fiction readers would naturally become acquainted with three categories of science fiction. First would be the New Wave, which I discovered by reading Harlan Ellison's *Dangerous Visions* anthology. Second would be hard science fiction, which I became aware of as a category from the example of Larry Niven. Finally would be fantasy, which became a prominent presence in science fiction due to the popularity of the paperback reprints of J. R. R. Tolkien in the mid-1960s. By the 1970s, people of this generation were emerging as science fiction fans and commentators; and with such memories, what could be more natural for them than to see science fiction as a genre divided into hard science fiction, New Wave or soft science fiction, and fantasy?

Therefore, all such dichotomies can be dismissed, in my view, as hopelessly time-bound—a fossilized record of perceptions of science fiction in the 1960s and 1970s, not of the true nature of the genre. Support for that argument is readily provided by the most prominent literary movement in science fiction of the 1980s, the cyberpunks. By virtue of their knowledge of, and extreme concern with, new forms of technology, many cyberpunks would have to be placed in the broad category of *hard science fiction*; yet their liberal politics, interest in literary experimentation, and polished style and characterization would place them in the broad category of *soft science fiction*. Bruce Sterling, the leading cyberpunk spokesman, would accept this viewpoint, since he once asserted that "what cyberpunk represents is an integration of New Wave and Hard SF" (Interview with Tayayuki Tatsumi 27). The cyberpunks therefore represent a fusion of *hard science fiction* and *soft science fiction* that is impossible to account for with these broad taxonomies.

Having some sense of what the term characteristically means, and some idea as to when and why the subgenre emerged, one may appropriately begin to examine a few key texts of hard science fiction. One obvious test case would be the work that was, in early comments on hard science fiction, most frequently associated with the term: Arthur C. Clarke's *A Fall of Moondust* (1961).

NOTES

1. This might also serve as an objection to seeing Stanislaw Lem as a hard science fiction writer, despite efforts to cast him as a key figure "in the vanguard of hard SF today" (Slusser and Rabkin, "Introduction" xiii)—as in George Guffey's "Noise, Information, and Statistics in Stanislaw Lem's *The Investigation*" and Robert Philmus's "The Cybernetic Paradigms of Stanislaw Lem," two essays in *Hard Science Fiction*.

2. One could also argue that Verne's cautious predictions were only examples of microcosmic hard science fiction, not macrocosmic hard science fiction; at best, then, Verne originated only one type of hard science fiction.

3. Of course, Gernsback was also getting reactions of a different kind from readers who complained about scientific data: one wrote, "Do not sacrifice story interest to scientific detail. (Why not block the very technical parts off in small type?)" ("The Reader Speaks" 92). Another was indifferent to questionable science: "Feeling, as I do, that the stories' chief aim is to amuse, and if possible to also impart a little information or stir the imagination ... I do not see the need for insisting that 'The Crystal Egg' is workable" ("Discussions," January 1927 974). Arguments about the importance of scientific accuracy in these letters anticipate the modern "hard vs. soft sf" debate, as Stephen P. Brown put it (Letter to Gary Westfahl). For more about Gernsback's ideas and how they affected contemporary authors and readers, see my "An Idea of Significant Import"; the ideas and role of John W. Campbell, Jr., mentioned below, are discussed in my "A Convenient Analog System."

4. Indeed, Gernsback's concept has now been realized, though the "magnetic storm" available today works by a different method: the explosion of a special nuclear bomb generates the magnetic energy that disables equipment. While little attention has been paid to this weapon, Norman Schwarzkopf proposed using the bomb during the Gulf War, though he was overruled.

5. A meteorite is a large rock that lands on Earth, a meteor is a rock that burns up while falling toward Earth, a meteoroid is a rock in space, and an asteroid is a large rock in space. Therefore, what van Vogt described should be called a "meteoroid station" or "asteroid station." Other critics have noticed this error.

6. Many of these works are described in my *Islands in the Sky* and listed in the bibliography *The Other Side of the Sky*.

7. In light of this, it is simply astonishing that James Blish, who was reading and writing science fiction at the time, should say in 1962 that "American science fiction [of the 1940s] was almost entirely 'hard'"—though he immediately backtracked a bit to say "[T]he *best* writers of that decade tried to be as respectful of the facts as Wells had been" ("Science-Fantasy and Translations" 103; my italics).

6

"He Was Part of Mankind": Arthur C. Clarke's *A Fall of Moondust*

Works like Arthur C. Clarke's *A Fall of Moondust*—microcosmic hard science fiction—are rarely examined by science fiction critics, even those with a special interest in hard science fiction. Brian W. Aldiss's *Trillion Year Spree* dismisses the novel in two sentences: "There the characters were embarrassingly wooden. Engineers dominated the proceedings, and the only problems were engineering problems" (401). Peter Nicholls's entry on Clarke in *The Science Fiction Encyclopedia* simply describes the novel as "a realistic account of an accident to a surface transport on a lightly colonized Moon" ("Arthur C. Clarke" 122). George Slusser's *The Space Odysseys of Arthur C. Clarke* does not even mention the novel, and two more complete surveys of Clarke's fiction—Eric S. Rabkin's *Arthur C. Clarke* and John Hollow's *Against the Night, the Stars: The Science Fiction of Arthur C. Clarke*—devote only a few pages to *A Fall of Moondust*, while spending more time discussing works like *Childhood's End, 2001: A Space Odyssey*, and *Rendezvous with Rama*.

The unstated and stated reasons for this relative neglect seem plain enough: In contrast to imaginative efforts to construct bizarre new environments, near-future adventures that take place in the space near Earth or on other planets of the solar system, adventures solidly built on reliable data, must be rather dull and prosaic. Such stories are said to emphasize machines and engineering rather than human beings, and may be dominated by what Ellison termed "shop talk." Indeed, these works may be said to celebrate technology at the expense of human values, and therefore be trivial, as Ellison indicates when he charges that "the hacks .... give us a nice technological thing that we can play with and toy with and masturbate with and we like that a lot" ("A Time for Daring" 113).

However, none of these judgments really apply to *A Fall of Moondust*.

It is true, first of all, that Clarke takes his readers to a very familiar place indeed—the moon, the locale of thousands of previous science fiction stories, and a place which had been stripped of most of its mysteries long before men walked on its surface. Yet in the opening pages of the novel, Clarke works hard to use the available data to demonstrate that the moon is indeed a strange new world. As the moonboat *Selene* travels to the Sea of Thirst, Clarke calls it "a sea of dust, not of water .... alien to all the experience of men .... neither land nor sea, neither air nor space" (4, 6). Clarke mentions the "illusion" that the lunar surface was "absolutely flat, and stretches to infinity" (6). They reach the Mountains of Inaccessibility— "a deeper mystery. Rising like an island out of the strange sea" (12). When the boat's lights are turned off, "The eye ... lost itself in a glittering maze" (12); then, "the travelers realized that not all the wonder lay in the sky. Behind the speeding cruiser stretched a long, phosphorescent wake, as if a magic finger had traced a line of light across the Moon's dark and dusty face" (13). When they look at a crater with floodlights, "it belonged to the kingdom of fantasy, as if ... from the haunted brain of Edgar Allan Poe" (15). The moon, according to Clarke, is alien, strange, magic, haunted; an illusion, a maze, a fantasy. Yet, with prosaic explanations mingled with the awestruck description, Clarke emphasizes that this picture of the moon is derived from the best scientific information available at the time.

And this brings up one interesting point about hard science fiction writers. There is a school of thought in science fiction that the accumulation of accurate data about the planets of the solar system, and the development of hardware that takes people and machines into that space, represents a tremendous loss, as the cold facts negate and eliminate the extravagant possibilities of earlier science fiction. Thus, Aldiss calls his anthology of stories about Venus *Farewell, Fantastic Venus!* (published in America as *All about Venus*) and there is an elegiac tone in Brian Stableford's conclusion that "We know now that the Mars of sf—in all its guises—has been nothing more than a dream" ("Mars" 383). Poul Anderson has described several writers' reactions to new discoveries about the planet Jupiter:

I remember sitting next to Jerry Pournelle at a meeting of the American Association for the Advancement of Science quite a few years ago, when the findings of the Pioneer One mission to Jupiter were first publicly described. Afterward we compared notes and found we had been thinking the same thing. As one revolutionary discovery after another came forth, we had thought: "There goes *Farmer in the Sky*. There goes 'Meeting with Medusa.' There goes 'Desertion.' There goes 'Call Me Joe.' There goes 'Bridge.'" And so on for every memorable story every written about Jupiter. ("Nature: Laws and Surprises" 8)

True facts about the solar system, then, seem to intolerably constrain the author's imaginative vistas, eliminating many exciting possibilities, so that writers are driven away from nearby space to write about distant solar systems, future Earth societies, or "inner space."

However, to hard science fiction writers, scientific facts are more interesting than fiction, and they want as many facts as possible in order to construct their future environments. Thus, Anderson concludes his apparently regretful remarks about Pioneer One's data on an upbeat note by saying, "Meanwhile, here we have been presented with this whole absolutely wonderful new world to write new stories about" (8). *A Fall of Moondust* argues that the actual nature of the moon is far more unusual and interesting than the world of H. G. Wells's Selenites or Edgar Rice Burroughs's Moon Men. In contrast to the others' laments, Clarke is always anxious to obtain more information about other worlds, so that he can write better stories about them. In the "Author's Note" to *2061: Odyssey Three*, he says, "*2010* was made possible by the brilliantly successful Voyager flybys of Jupiter, and I had not intended to return to that territory until the results of the even more ambitious Galileo Mission were in .... Alas, the Challenger tragedy eliminated that scenario .... I have decided not to wait" (ix-x). From this perspective, humanity's improved information and growing access to outer space and other worlds is not constraining, but liberating, which explains why such stories have continued to thrive throughout the space age.

It thus seems that what might be termed the environmental imperative of macrocosmic hard science fiction is also present in its apparently less ambitious relatives. Sam Moskowitz has touched upon this aspect of all of Clarke's fiction: His "ideas are never introduced obliquely or discussed in a blasé, over-sophisticated, or matter-of-fact manner, a method indigenous in too much of modern science fiction. Instead, he vests them with all the poetry, wonder, awe, mystery, and adventure that he is capable of conjuring up. Even if it is only the preparation of the first space rocket, he attempts to communicate the richness and implication of an overwhelming experience" (*Seekers of Tomorrow* 391). Thus, hard science fiction writers like Clarke do not see the real solar system as dull and stifling; they still argue that such worlds are in fact infinitely strange and demand detailed exploration both in fact and in fiction; and manned and unmanned ventures into space have not diminished their interest in those realms, just as interest in the American West did not diminish the minute people began to settle there.[1]

Of course, Clarke is attentive both to the lunar environment and to the machines and equipment that people have devised to explore and inhabit that environment; and some passages in the novel do seem to reflect a fascination with technology and, as Aldiss charges, "engineering problems." The man in charge of the rescue mission is, after all, Chief Engineer Lawrence, and thinking of the low gravity and absence of an atmosphere, he calls the moon "an engineer's paradise" (135)—a statement that might have broader applications to the novel. Clarke describes the rapid creation and construction of rescue equipment: "[U]nsung and unrecorded miracles of improvisation .... A complete air-conditioning plant .... a small drilling rig .... specially designed plumbing"

(161). He pauses to marvel at the efficiency and speed of interplanetary communication: "In a sixth of a second [a radio pulse] had flashed the fifty thousand kilometers to the relay satellite known as Lagrange II .... Another sixth of a second and the pulse had returned, much amplified, flooding Earthside North .... The computer waited for another five seconds. Then it sent out the pulse again" (19-20). As such language seems to celebrate technology, the novel's plot might be said to convey the same message. Carefully, Clarke subjects the people of the *Selene* to four menaces, each involving the four elements of ancient alchemy: First, the lunar dust—a form of *earth*—engulfs the boat and leaves the passengers totally cut off from humanity; then the *air* in the boat starts to go bad, threatening to kill the passengers; next, the *water* discharged from the boat unsettles the dust beyond the boat and causes it to sink further; and finally, a *fire* breaks out in the boat.[2]   And each time, technology comes to the rescue: An astronomer with an infra-red detector finds the sunken boat; Chief Engineer Lawrence sinks an air tube into the boat to give the passengers fresh oxygen; after the boat sinks some more, Lawrence relocates it and reestablishes the oxygen connection; and he completes a connective tunnel and gets the passengers to safety just as the fire engulfs the vessel. Thus, it seems, the novel is the story of the triumph of technology over nature; John Hollow says the novel concerns "the battle between humanity and Nature" (*Against the Night, the Stars* 111), and Eric S. Rabkin says the novel "is the best example of a faith in science that runs throughout Clarke's fiction" (*Arthur C. Clarke* 19).[3]

But there is one problem with such readings of the novel: All of these problems were in fact *caused* by technology. The *Selene* is a boat, as Clarke announces in the first sentence of the novel, and any boat, no matter how safely it is designed, should carry with it a way to rescue passengers in case the boat sinks—lifeboats, life preservers, or at least signal flares. However, since the engineers who designed it thought sinking was impossible, they constructed no such provisions. As a result, as soon as the *Selene* sinks under the surface, its occupants find that the radio is useless, the vehicle has no way of announcing its location, and they have no way to make the boat rise again or to get out of the boat and rescue themselves. A more colossal failure of basic engineering cannot be imagined.

Second, the air goes bad because the system for removing carbon dioxide—based on "[s]traight chemical absorption"—is disabled by the heat the trapped vessel generates (138), another incredible blunder in design.

Third, because the *Selene* dumps out wastewater instead of recycling it, its forced motionlessness saturates the dust beneath it, causing instability and further sinking—yet another problem that should have been anticipated.

Finally, the boat's insulation catches fire because lunar dust creeps into the *Selene*, and since the dust had "enough meteoric iron ... to make it a good conductor," the dust "short[s] all the electrical equipment" (233); and of course, there are no fire extinguishers on board. The struggle in *A Fall of Moondust*, then, is not using technology to help people triumph over nature but *rescuing them from a technological death-trap.*

The message about technology in *A Fall of Moondust*, then, is ambivalent: Scientific progress will enable people to explore and inhabit unusual new worlds, but will do so in a way that creates problems and dangers requiring additional scientific ingenuity and effort to resolve. Hard science fiction clearly abhors a Luddite rejection of technology, but neither does it embrace a bland technophiliac optimism regarding the powers of technology.

In fact, even the mild optimism of this novel—the argument that technology can eventually triumph over the its own self-created pitfalls—does not entirely explain the attitude of hard science fiction; for in his more expansive moments Clarke offers a sense of cosmic futility regarding the ultimate effects of humanity's scientific progress. This feeling is prominent in the Clarke novel that most closely resembles *A Fall of Moondust, The Ghost from the Grand Banks.* Here again is the story of two disparate men coming together to rescue a sunken vessel; in this case, of course, the *Titanic* has long rested at the bottom of the ocean with its passengers beyond rescue, so the novel is the story of trying to raise the boat, not trying to save people. Still, since the *Titanic* stands as a premier example of the failure of technology, bringing it up to the surface would serve as a belated and symbolic reaffirmation of the power of technology to deal with its own mistakes.

However, the effort to return the *Titanic* fails when a massive underwater upheaval disrupts retrieval operations and makes the ship permanently inaccessible; and a coda to the story describes an alien spaceship, visiting the Earth long after humanity is gone, beginning its own effort to raise the *Titanic*—an attempt that the text clearly implies will be equally futile. One might argue that Clarke blandly mentioned a restored *Titanic* in his earlier *Imperial Earth* and that *The Ghost from the Grand Banks* simply represents a late surge of pessimism; still, the example demonstrates that a celebratory attitude toward all aspects of technological progress, and a blind "faith in science," is hardly intrinsic to hard science fiction.

Even if a certain degree of flexibility and skepticism is granted in works of hard science fiction, there remains the charge that in their emphasis on technology, such works can neglect human values—and human characters. If one pays attention only to the trapped passengers in *A Fall of Moondust*, the accusation seems valid, since the people depicted there are uniformly flat—as noted, Aldiss calls them "wooden," and Rabkin says, "The cast of characters is as stereotypically drawn as in any disaster movie" (*Arthur C. Clarke* 63)—and their escapades and revelations are generally tiresome and uninteresting. However, since their first activity after realizing their plight is to form an Entertainment Committee, and since they spend most of their time performing a staged novel reading and participating in a mock trial, Clarke suggests that these cardboard figures should be regarded as entertainment—a sideshow, a diversion; the true story of *A Fall of Moondust* is the story of the people who rescue the *Selene*. And the two men who are primarily responsible for that rescue are more noteworthy and less "stereotypical."

As the novel begins, astronomer Andy Lawson is described as an orphan who was victimized by an abusive childhood, only to be saved when his brilliance earned him a scholarship. He works alone in a space station, misanthropic, isolated, irascible; here is one problem in the novel that is not an "engineering problem." Less is said about Chief Engineer Lawrence, but he, too, seems cold and inhuman, totally preoccupied by the tasks at hand.

However, both men are changed when they go out together to the Sea of Thirst to search for signs of the missing boat. Unfamiliar with the lunar environment, Lawson at one point seems about to panic; Lawrence talks to him and calms him down. Afterwards, Clarke describes their feelings: "[T]he astronomer sat quite motionless ... apparently listening to some inner voice. What was it telling him? wondered Lawrence. Perhaps that he was part of mankind .... Perhaps that, somewhere in the world, there might be a person who could care for him and ... break through the ice that had encrusted his heart" (101). This odd epiphany, this powerful moment of human contact, is soon reinforced when Lawrence falls into the dust and momentarily panics about sinking into it (though he quickly realizes that there is no real danger). Lawson laughs at his plight, then quickly apologizes. Later, Lawrence reacts to the incident: "[H]is mixture of fright and anger slowly evaporated. It was replaced by a mood of thoughtfulness, as he realized how closely—whether he liked it or not—the events of the last half-hour had linked him with Lawson" (110-111). Virtual strangers, standing on the lunar surface in space suits, these two men brought together by a technological disaster are somehow "linked"; and after this experience, both men change considerably. Lawson is repeatedly interviewed by television newsmen about the crisis and, while retaining an edginess of sorts, grows talkative and personable, eventually becoming a popular television personality. Seeing him so accessible on the air, one of his colleagues remarks, "frankly ... I would never have recognized him" (142). Less dramatically, Lawrence starts to act more like a human being, finally agreeing to an interview with the newsman covering the rescue operation. Hard science fiction is often accused of having technology turn human beings into robots; but in this book, technology seems to turn robots into human beings.

Indeed, almost all the scientific energies expended in the novel can be interpreted as attempts to bring people together, to establish contact between people and thereby make them more human. That is the very enterprise of the mission itself—first establishing radio contact, then connecting an oxygen tube to the trapped boat, and finally building a tunnel that links the boat to the surface. There are repeated references to the power of instantaneous television contact, including the news reports on the rescue mission and the teleconference presided over by Lawrence that decides how to proceed with the rescue. In the process of creating problems that people must solve, and in bringing together people who are concerned about those problems, technology paradoxically becomes a humanizing force.[4]

For these reasons, it is hard to accept Eric S. Rabkin's reading of the novel as "a work which ignores vision for the sake of pure scientific thinking," a novel that "revolves around such matters of science and our reactions to it" and where the major attraction is "the suspenseful unfolding of scientific detail" (*Arthur C. Clarke* 19, 37). The scientific thinking that went into the construction of the *Selene*, after all, was amazingly sloppy, and Clarke contrives to "humanize" not only scientific "thinking"—as Rabkin claims (*Arthur C. Clarke* 19)—but also his characters Lawson and Lawrence.[5]

This brings up one issue: Many critics see a stark conflict in hard science fiction between human desires and scientific realities. Because it celebrates the primacy of science, hard science fiction is "cold," inhuman, and threatening to traditional humanistic values. The argument originated with John W. Campbell, Jr., in his article "Science Fiction and the Opinion of the Universe":

Where classical values hold that human nature is enduring, unchanging, and uniform [he argued], science-fiction holds that it is mutable, complex, and differentiated. David Riesman ... has suggested that there are three basic personality types: the Tradition-Directed man, the Inner-Directed, and the Other-Directed. But there's a fourth type that only *appears* to be Inner-Directed. Let's call it the Universe-Directed type .... The Universe-Directed type isn't ruled by opinions—he's dominated by the facts of the Universe .... The scientist will appear from the viewpoint of someone who considers opinion the dominant force in reality—rigid, cold-blooded, emotionless, and authoritarian-dogmatic. He isn't; the Universe is, and he's acting simply as the messenger of the Universe. Accusing the scientist of being cold-blooded or dogmatic is somewhat like the king who had the messenger beheaded for bringing the news that the battle had been lost. (10)

And some later critics have echoed this opinion, especially regarding hard science fiction; consider, for example, the comments of George Slusser and Eric S. Rabkin in the introduction to their anthology *Hard Science Fiction*:

The method then of the hard SF story is logical, the means technological, and the result—the feel and texture of the fiction itself—objective and cold. What hard SF purports to affirm, therefore, is not the universality of human aspirations, for these are more often than not the "soft" products of our desires. Instead it asserts the truth of natural law, an absolute, seeming ahuman vision of things. Such a vision may seem to run counter to the humanist tradition, to the basically man-centered structures of Western literature itself. ("Introduction" vii)

In continuing his argument, Campbell, also much like later critics, offers the example of Tom Godwin's "The Cold Equations," a story about the pilot of a space rescue mission who is unhappily forced to jettison and kill a stowaway because his ship's exactly calculated fuel supply cannot safely carry her extra weight. That story—unsurprisingly heavily influenced and published by Campbell—includes rhetoric that echoes Campbell's and Slusser and Rabkin's description of the fundamental ethos of hard science fiction:

Existence required Order and there was Order; the laws of nature, irrevocable and immutable. Men could learn to use them, but men could not change them. The circumference of a circle was always pi times the diameter and no science of Man would ever make it otherwise. The combination of chemical A with chemical B under condition C invariably produced reaction D. The law of gravitation was a rigid equation and it made no distinction between the fall of a leaf and the ponderous circling of a binary star system. The nuclear conversion process powered the cruisers that carried men to the stars; the same process in the form of a nova would destroy a world with equal efficiency. The laws *were*, and the universe moved in obedience to them. Along the frontier were arrayed all the forces of nature, and sometimes they destroyed those who were fighting their way outward from Earth. The men of the frontier had long ago learned the bitter futility of cursing the forces that would destroy them for the forces were blind and deaf; the futility of looking to the heavens for mercy, for the stars of the galaxy swung in their long, long sweep of two hundred million years, as inexorably controlled as they by the laws that knew neither hatred nor compassion. (559)

Others have argued that "The Cold Equations" represents the true nature of hard science fiction. John Huntington called it "a classic hard-core SF work .... This quintessential hard-core story .... our paradigmatic story" ("Hard-Core Science Fiction and the Illusion of Science" 45, 52, 56); and James Gunn echoed that judgment by defining it as a "touchstone story because if readers don't understand it they don't understand science fiction. The intellectual point made by the story is that sentimentality divorced from knowledge and rationality is deadly" ("The Readers of Hard Science Fiction" 72). Thus, a story regularly accepted as hard science fiction is seen as a virtual definition of the genre, the purest and most powerful expression of its central message.

I see a number of problems in this argument.

First of all, Campbell's attitude seems to reflect a view of science that is at least a century out of date. The four nouns that define modern physics are *relativity*, *probability*, *uncertainty*, and *chaos*. We no longer see Newton's clockwork universe, but rather one that is surprisingly unpredictable, illogical, even whimsical; and in contemplating a universe where particles simultaneously exist and do not exist, where our eleven-dimensional universe seems four-dimensional because seven of those dimensions are wrapped in little bundles inside those particles, adjectives like *immutable* and *inexorable* no longer seem to apply. Instead, one must conclude that the nineteenth-century thinker who most accurately anticipated modern physics was not Lord Kelvin but Lewis Carroll. Clarke, who keeps up with recent developments, captures this new sense of physical reality by building into *The Ghost from the Grand Banks* the image of the Mandelbrot Set, an extremely simple algorithm that generates a curve of literally infinite complexity, that becomes more and more convoluted the more closely one examines it. Simply put, the equations scientists confront today are not always particularly cold; they may be lively and surprising.

What is paraded as a "scientific" attitude should be seen as a crude negation of humanistic values—which overly simplifies matters.[6] The picture of the universe science offers today is not particularly cold and mechanical; nor is it warm and cuddly. Rather, instead of negating or confirming human expectations, the modern universe is simply *different* than human expectations.

A second problem with this argument is how frequently "The Cold Equations" is used to exemplify it. If this "scientific" viewpoint is in fact so prevalent in hard science fiction, there should be numerous stories with that viewpoint; the fact that critics keep returning to Godwin's story suggests that it is in fact more of an aberration than a representative example.[7]

The third—and most important—problem with this attitude is that "The Cold Equations" actually represents the triumph of an attitude *exactly opposite to the one Campbell presents*, because Godwin originally wrote the story so that the girl survived. This interesting fact, noted by James Gunn in the question-and-answer session after a talk at the Fifth Eaton Conference, was confirmed by Campbell himself in a 1969 letter:

Only once did I send a story back six times for revisions—and that was not a commissioned story, but an author who had an idea, a good one, and could write—but simply couldn't accept the underlying honest answer to the story-idea he had come up with. "The Cold Equations" by Tom Godwin is now one of the classic shorts of science fiction. It was Tom's idea, and he wrote every word of it, and sweated over it ... because he just simply couldn't accept that the *girl simply had to die.* (Letter to Ronald E. Graham 86)

As this letter reveals, Godwin was in actuality incredibly stubborn in wishing to have his heroine survive; Campbell literally had to demand six rewrites in order to force Godwin to provide the preferred conclusion. And since he long maintained that attitude despite his natural desire to sell his story, Godwin's commitment to human values, not scientific principles, appears even more remarkable.[8]

One can imagine what "The Cold Equations" was like in its original form. The beginning of the story was the same: The man discovers the girl stowaway and reluctantly tells her that the cold equations of motion mean that she has to die. But Godwin's hero originally did not leave it at that; he kept studying those cold equations and eventually he thought of some new possibility, some loophole, and he figured out a way to save the girl's life. And that impulse—the determination to push and twist scientific reality to meet human needs—is, I submit, what actually defines both practical science and hard science fiction.

Perhaps "The Cold Equations" is historically important in that it demonstrated the potential for novelty in science fiction; however, the story remains fundamentally illogical. To see what is wrong with Godwin's story, translate it into a realistic story: A pilot gets into a small airplane to fly needed medical supplies to a remote outpost; he discovers a girl has stowed away in the plane; he announces that if the plane continues to bear her excess weight, it will not be able to reach its destination; so he pushes her out the window. What's wrong with this story? *This is not the way airplanes are designed.* Yes, airplanes are designed to carry a certain weight, but they are also engineered so that they can fly with some excess weight; yes, airplanes are designed to carry enough fuel to reach a certain destination, but they also can carry extra fuel in case of emergencies.

Even dealing with the more exacting parameters of space flight, reasonable engineers would always build such "fudge factors" into their equipment. Thus, there seems to be little sense in the economic argument that Godwin attempts to build for his precisely calculated spaceships: "The cruisers were forced by necessity to carry a limited amount of the bulky rocket fuel and the fuel was rationed with care; the cruiser's computers determining the exact amount of fuel each [spaceship] would require for its mission. The computers considered the course coordinates, the mass of the EDS, the mass of pilot and cargo; they were very precise and omitted nothing from their calculations" (544). Again, though, imagine what would happen if some airplane company, due to dire economic necessity, began sending out aircraft with only the exact amount of fuel their flights would require and nothing more; because human beings are not perfect, there would always be slight discrepancies in weight measurement, unexpected course adjustments, pilot mistakes, and the like, and airplanes would start crashing with alarming regularity. It thus makes much more economic sense to provide some extra fuel, some margin for error, to allow for these inevitable problems. The same would be true for Godwin's Emergency Dispatch Ships: Every time a mistake occurred, a ship would be destroyed, and no company could long tolerate such a disastrous situation.

In short, no intelligent space-faring civilization would ever design and fly a spaceship that becomes dysfunctional if an extra hundred pounds or so are on board; thus, "The Cold Equations" may be a story of good physics, but it is also a story of lousy engineering.[9]

I should add that John Huntington's "Hard-Core Science Fiction and the Illusion of Science" attacks the logic of "The Cold Equations" from another angle: That the men of the story "never try to improvise some mode of salvation for her" (56). "Throughout the story," he notes, "items have been mentioned on the spaceship that are dispensable: there is the door of the closet, the blaster, the people's clothes, the pilot's chair, the closet itself, its contents, the senser [*sic*] that registers body heat, the bench she sits on ... Do they need the radio any more? ... [N]o one even begins to consider such possibilities" (52; first ellipses author's; second ellipses mine). One might combine the arguments to say that a well-engineered spaceship should, among other things, have a built-in capacity to reduce its weight to respond to emergency conditions. Overall, I suspect that there are many other logical errors in the scenario of "The Cold Equations"; for example, if the computers on board the cruisers are capable of calculating to the exact ounce how much the EDS will weigh and how much fuel it will require, why were they incapable of noticing that the ship had the extra weight of a stowaway until after the ship was launched?

As already established, *A Fall of Moondust* is also to an extent a story of lousy engineering; but it is also the story of a powerful impulse to ignore scientific logic and overcome limited technology to fulfill human needs. If Clarke's heroes, like Campbell's scientist and Godwin's pilot, had been content to study the cold equations and accept their dictates, the people on board the *Selene* would not have been saved. After the initial disaster, one scientist logically concludes that the *Selene* must have been buried in a landslide and that search-and-rescue efforts are therefore futile; only Lawson's stubbornness leads him to continue the infrared search that eventually shows where the *Selene* actually vanished. When Lawson first arrives at the Sea of Thirst, the readings he gets are all chaotic, and he is ready to abandon the effort as hopeless; but Lawrence tells him to keep trying, and they eventually find that in the designated area the readings are patterned and accurate. After setting up a schedule for putting an air tube down to the boat, Lawrence learns that the air in the boat is going bad and will kill the passengers before the tube is connected; Lawrence accelerates the schedule and gets it there in time. And the passengers, instead of meekly accepting their doom, employ tranquilizers and an emergency air supply to keep themselves alive for as long as possible, just in case Lawrence can complete the task in time. When the ship shifts a little further down and into a slanted position, the connecting tunnel can no longer be attached to the roof in any way; so Lawrence devises a way to do it. The fire is sure to engulf the boat before the tunnel is connected; but the fire is delayed just long enough to get the tunnel connected and the passengers out safely.

A Fall of Moondust suggests, therefore, that despite an apparent emphasis on technology, microcosmic hard science fiction is in fact dedicated to supporting and accommodating human values, even in the face of scientific logic.[10] However, the argument that hard science fiction has a hidden agenda oriented to human values may sound very much like a truism; after all, stories that are written by and for human beings must inevitably reflect human attitudes to a large extent, as science fiction writer Stanislaw Lem has often pointed out. But in science fiction, this is not always the case.

Ever since Hugo Gernsback demanded that science fiction be firmly based on scientific fact, and ever since John W. Campbell, Jr., demanded that science fiction be developed through scientific thinking, there has existed the possibility of writing a story that would confound all traditional expectations. The process was outlined by Campbell:

[T]hat's the fun of science-fiction writing; the plotting is as nearly 100% uninhibited as anything imaginable. If an idea doesn't fit in with conditions of Earth, you're free to invent a planet where it will fit—so long as you don't defy some obvious law of Nature .... you can set up a world to play with as you like. You can consider any social structure you like, carried to any extreme you need, to bring out your points. One thing, and one thing only, is properly demanded of the story, once its reasonable premise is set forth: the story must be self-consistent from there on. Then, science-fiction is the freest, least formalized of any literary medium. In this field, the reader can never be sure just how the author may wind up—and because the author feels that freedom, he can let the story have its head, let it develop in any direction that the logic of the developing situation may dictate. Many times a story actually winds up entirely different from the idea with which the author started. And, very rarely, an author can simply start a story, and let it work its own way out to a conclusion! ("Introduction" to *Who Goes There?* 5-6)

And occasional science fiction stories do seem to reflect this process and its possibilities. Heinlein regularly began stories without knowing how they would end, and "Solution Unsatisfactory" and "Goldfish Bowl" both follow their premises to unpalatable and unusual conclusions. Piers Anthony and Robert E. Margroff's *The Ring* begins like a conventional warning against the dangers of mind-control as a way to prevent crime, like Anthony Burgess's *A Clockwork Orange*; but as the story develops, the protagonist discovers that he actually likes wearing a Ring to limit his behavior, and the novel becomes a qualified argument for some forms of mind control. Works like Damon Knight's "Stranger Station," Terry Carr's "The Dance of the Changer and the Three" and Clifford D. Simak's *The Visitors* create aliens and refuse to either sentimentalize or demonize them; they remain strange and inexplicable. Of course, except for Heinlein, none of these writers are usually associated with hard science fiction—which is the point; the possibility of such stories is part of the general heritage of the genre and not only a result of the techniques of hard science fiction.

To be sure, there is an exploratory and experimental element in creating hard science fiction, as Robert F. Forward explains, and there are stories in the subgenre that reach unsettling conclusions, like Clarke's *Childhood's End* and Charles Sheffield's *Between the Strokes of Night*, two novels that seem driven to the conclusion that there is some incompatibility between conquering the universe and remaining human, but unable to decide exactly where their sympathies lie. However, in some ways, the process of writing hard science fiction is inimicable to such challenging and unexpected results.

To explore hard science fiction as a flawed scientific experiment, first reduce the scientific method to these basics: The scientist suspects that a certain experiment will have certain results; she sets up and carries out that experiment; then she observes and records the actual results. Say that there are two theoretical models for writing science fiction in a scientific manner—Clement's and Campbell's. In Clement's method, the writer envisions a certain type of world, then works with scientific data and logic to produce such a world. The problem here is obvious: The same person is setting up the experiment and generating all the data, so there is inevitable bias in the proceedings; as noted, writers constructing fictional worlds, whenever they have a choice, invariably choose results that make the world more favorable to humans and human adventures, so in spite of their best intentions, they may not notice or explore other interesting consequences of their work.

Campbell's method eliminates that problem by demanding that the writer begin with an open mind, with no conclusion in mind, so the writer can follow the thought-experiment wherever it leads; that process may therefore lead to more genuinely unexpected and unsettling stories. But this also is not the way scientists work; a hypothesis always precedes the experiment, and no chemist, for example, ever spends time randomly mixing chemicals together to see if anything interesting happens.

A true application of the scientific method to the process of writing science fiction, then, might involve the following: One writer imagines that certain posited inventions or conditions might have certain results, so she gives the data to another writer without revealing what results she anticipates; the other writer then writes a story based on those data; then the original writer observes the results and compares them to what she anticipated. This would be an improvement on Clement's method, since here there would be different people setting up the experiment and generating the data, and an improvement on Campbell's method, since there would be an expected result that could be compared to actual results.

If this model is accepted as a logical approach, the best available example of writing in a scientific manner would be collaborative projects like Harlan Ellison's *Medea: Harlan's World*; and the way Ellison laid the groundwork for that anthology is interesting. First, he asked three prominent hard science fiction writers—Hal Clement, Poul Anderson, and Larry Niven—to work up a detailed picture of the astronomical location, physical characteristics, and biology of an imaginary world called Medea; a fourth writer, Frederik Pohl, was brought in to offer some thoughts on its politics, sociology, and other issues. Then, their materials were presented to four other writers—Theodore Sturgeon, Robert Silverberg, Thomas M. Disch, and Frank Herbert—at a dinner meeting; two hours later, the men participated in a public discussion about what sorts of stories might be developed involving that world. Later, all eight of these writers—along with Ellison and two other writers, Jack Williamson and Kate Wilhelm—wrote stories about Medea. In some ways, the project resembles what I suggested: One set of writers developing a scientific background, another set of writers developing stories employing that background. But there are two differences. First, the process did not feature the strict separation of creator and writer that I argued was necessary; some of the creators offered story ideas, some of the writers added some background information, and everyone eventually participated in the story-writing. Second, the purpose of this project was not to test any hypothesis regarding hard science fiction but simply to allow students in the class to observe the creative process in action: Ellison announces, "[T]his singular project called Medea is a step-by-step *modus operandum* demonstrating not only *where* the ideas comes from, but what one does with them once they've manifested themselves." And he invites particular attention to the creative step from background to story—"Part of the game of this book will be your trying to find the germinal moments of scattergun thinking that eventually resulted in the stories actually written by these four [authors]" ("Cosmic Hod-Carriers" 1,4). Still, the process Ellison set up could be easily adapted to perform an experimental test of hard science fiction as a scientific experiment.[11]

In any event, one conclusion from my analysis here is that Arthur C. Clarke's *A Fall of Moondust* cannot be regarded as a true product of a scientific thought-experiment. Indeed, we can finally see that the novel has been fundamentally misinterpreted: Grudgingly or enthusiastically admired as a precise thought-experiment in scientific logic, the novel is actually highly suspect as a projection of future technology; condemned for its inattentiveness or hostility to human values, the novel is actually deeply committed to an affirmation of those values. It is time, then, to shake the dust off our traditional attitudes toward hard science fiction.[12]

NOTES

1. Clarke brings up the analogy when the passengers at one point are reading aloud from a scholarly discussion of the connection "between the Old West and the New Space" (62-63).

2. One could argue there was a fifth danger, an initial fear of overheating; but this turns out to be a simple miscalculation: The scientist who figured out that the heat would rise to intolerable levels did not take into account the boat's radiator fans, so the heat stabilized, with no need for corrective action. The other four dangers, however, were real, and demanded corrective action.

3. In documenting his interpretation, Hollow cites a few statements from characters indicating that they have "long held pictures of themselves as locked in a

battle with Nature" (110); and certainly, any novel about lunar exploration and colonization must involve some mention of this theme. However, as I will argue, it is very difficult to see the particular action of this novel as a battle against nature.

4. Hollow does capture this aspect of the novel when he says, "[T]he novel certainly insists that the people are rescued by other people" (*Against the Night, the Stars* 110).

5. In fairness to Rabkin, he does seem to back away from these and other judgments about Clarke's works in the final passage of his study: "[W]hat Clarke writes may appear to be about science, appear to be about numbers, appear to be about ideas, but in fact at bottom whatever Clarke writes is about people and that means that it is about the human spirit" (*Arthur C. Clarke* 60).

6. The point was made years ago by Reginald Bretnor:

[W]e generally accept the old Aristotelian scheme, in which the "warm, spontaneous emotions" and "the cold, logical intellect" are assumed to function separately, like two frogs jumping in a basket .... That "science" is opposed to "the emotions," and that somehow it is inimical to "human nature." ...

The scientific method, then, is a process composed of certain other processes. The important point is that it occurs *inside human beings* .... [I]ts formulation did not constitute a new invention, but was instead simply an awakening to the fact of its existence—the recognition of a perfectly normal human function built into every normal human being.

The scientific method is human, and purely human, and wholly human. To say that it is not, to say that it is somehow extra-human or anti-human, is to misrepresent reality. ("The Future of Science Fiction" 270-271)

7. Critics who wish to see Godwin's story as "paradigmatic" should accept this simple challenge: Locate five other stories in modern science fiction that are similar to it. I suspect they could not meet that challenge.

8. Incidentally, since Gunn knew that the story's original form was significantly different from its published version, it is surprising that he would later define the work as "a touchstone story."

9. To me, Gunn concedes the essential illogic in the story when he says:

"The Cold Equations" could have been told only as science fiction, not because the point of the story is science fiction, but because every other situation retains an element of hope for rescue. In a contemporary lifeboat story or a story about wagon trains crossing the plains, the sacrifice of an innocent stowaway to save the lives of the remainder brings up images of the Donner party; the point of those stories would be the survivors' lack of faith and their love of life above honor. Science fiction gave Godwin an unparalleled opportunity to purify the situation in such a way that there was no hope left for last-minute salvation, no possible sight of land or rescue ship, no company of soldiers to ride over the hill. ("The Readers of Hard Science Fiction" 72)

However, if people plan their lives in inhospitable places on Earth in a way that always allows for the possibility of rescue, why should they plan their lives differently when they venture into outer space?

10. Norman Spinrad, after analyzing novels by Greg Bear and Gregory Benford, reaches a somewhat similar conclusion: He says Bear's *The Forge of God* shows "that *humanistic hard science fiction* need not be a contradiction in terms," and that "[t]he best so-called 'hard science fiction writers' like Benford know in their heart of hearts that the[y] must give and bend a bit in the service of total literary concerns, whether they are willing to admit it in polite company or not" ("The Hard Stuff" 100, 108).

11. Ellison does mention two previous anthologies of a similar nature—Fletcher Platt's *The Petrified Planet* and Roger Elwood's *A World Named Cleopatra*.

12. In "The Case against Space," I analyze the arguments advanced for human space exploration in fiction and nonfiction by hard science fiction writers like Ben Bova, Jerry Pournelle, and G. Harry Stine [Lee Correy] to reach a similar conclusion: That these writers are being guided more by their human aspirations than their scientific data.

7

"Like Something Living":
Hal Clement's *Mission of Gravity*

Looking at Hal Clement's *Mission of Gravity*, one immediately sees there is a reason other than sheer scale for distinguishing stories of this type— macrocosmic hard science fiction—from the microcosmic variety: namely, different generic models.

Set in the near-future, with near-future technology, the microcosmic hard science fiction story naturally lends itself to a number of story patterns involving present-day people and present-day technology. Clarke's *A Fall of Moondust* adopts the form of the disaster-and-rescue story—Hollow notes it is "really a version of the mine-disaster story" (*Against the Night, the Stars* 110)—as does Godwin's "The Cold Equations" and Martin Caidin's *Marooned*; others—like Clarke's *Earthlight* and George Bishop's *The Shuttle People*—follow the pattern of detective fiction; Clarke's "The Wind from the Sun" is essentially a sports story in space; while James P. Hogan's *Endgame Enigma* and Ben Bova's *Colony* are spy thrillers writ large.

However, stories like *Mission of Gravity* necessarily gravitate, so to speak, toward another generic model: the travel tale. When a hard science fiction writer faces the challenge of presenting a vast or unusual new world to readers, the most obvious narrative pattern would be to feature explorers making their way through this new world, gradually learning about its characteristics and features. Certainly, novels like Clarke's *Rendezvous with Rama* and Larry Niven's *Ringworld* take this form.

This is also the pattern of *Mission of Gravity*, which at its heart is the story of brave explorers who must traverse a bizarre new world in order to retrieve an important space probe; Poul Anderson described the book as "a wonderful travelogue through an imaginary planet" (Interview with Jeffrey M. Elliot 43); John Clute called it "a continuously fascinating ecological travelogue" ("Hal Clement" 123); and Gregory Benford said it was "an epic odyssey across this planet led by the tiny natives" ("Science and Science Fiction" 32).

However, Clement's Mesklin did pose a special challenge. The most natural approach would be to feature human explorers encountering the new world, as is seen in *Rendezvous with Rama* and *Ringworld*; however, because of its immense gravity, humans can survive only on the extreme edge of the planet. And the obvious alternative of employing native inhabitants as protagonists may be flawed: How can beings explore with a genuine sense of interest the world they already live in? Clement's solution is twofold: First, he uses Mesklinites as his heroes but has them venture into regions of the world that are unknown to them, thus maintaining their stance as pioneering advernturers; second, by keeping the Mesklinites in constant radio contact with humans, he maintains a human viewpoint in the picture. As each new aspect of Mesklin is revealed, then, there is always someone around to be surprised by it, someone whose startled reactions can parallel those of the readers.

The strategy works, in part, because the Mesklinites as Clement describes them are easy to identify with—something that is regularly seen as a flaw in the novel. That is, one might imagine that the task of creating exotic imaginary worlds would naturally lead a writer to create strange beings, strange stories, and strange ideas; but *Mission of Gravity* suggests that exactly the opposite occurs. George R. R. Martin recognized this tendency when he was advising prospective writers on how to create genuine aliens in science fiction:

Although world-building can be valid and effective, creating vivid backgrounds and realistic, well-considered aliens when used correctly, on the whole I do not think the method should be recommended .... The work of Hal Clement, one of the most practiced of the world-builders, points up some of those dangers .... [A]lthough Clement is often cited as being particularly good with aliens, actually the reverse is sometimes true .... The protagonists of the novel are Mesklinites, aliens admirably tailored to meet the physical conditions of their world in the best world-builder fashion .... Other than that, captain Barlennan of the good ship *Bree* and his crew are virtually human .... Clement fails in the last test—he has not bothered to create an *alien*. The world overshadows its inhabitants. ("First, Sew on a Tentacle" 157-158)

Others make the same charge: Peter Nicholls says the Mesklinites "are so different from us in appearance and environment as to be awe-inspiring, until they open their mouths, whereupon they sound exactly like Calvin Coolidge" ("Science Fiction: The Monsters and the Critics" 174); and David N. Samuelson claims, "The greatest weakness" in *Mission of Gravity* "is its characterization of its aliens. They look like centipedes with lobster claws, act and think like Renaissance sailors, and talk largely like '50s engineers, at least as they are represented in American SF" ("Modes of Extrapolation" 205). There is some justice in these complaints: Since Mesklinites are, after all, foot-long centipede-like creatures who crawl on the ground in gravity hundreds of times greater than that of Earth, it is certainly incongruous that they should evolve cultural and economic systems that closely resemble those of Europe in the Middle Ages and that Barlennan's shrewdness and practicality are so humanlike.

Still, Barlennan is more than a human sea captain in disguise. Clement goes to some length to explain some of the unusual psychological reactions such beings might have; one key moment comes early in the novel when Barlennan's human companion Lackland casually *"picked up* the tiny body of the Mesklinite. For one soul-shaking instant Barlennan felt and saw himself suspended long feet away from the ground .... [H]is eyes glared in undiluted horror at the emptiness .... The fear might have—perhaps should have—driven him mad. His situation can only be dimly approximated by comparing it with that of a human being hanging by one hand from a window ledge forty stories above a paved street" (23). While Clement is ultimately driven to impose a human comparison on the experience, he is clearly striving to convey the fact that Mesklinites, by nature, do not always think and react like human beings—a point that is also made later when Barlennan must communicate with foreign Mesklinites who do not speak his language: "[H]is gestures were meaningless to Lackland .... How any understanding could be transmitted was a complete mystery .... [He] had not gained more than the tiniest bit of insight into their psychology .... So much of the Mesklinite action and gesticulation is tied in directly with the physical functioning of their bodies that its meaning, seen by another member of the same race, is automatically clear" (64-65). Despite such moments, one can concede Martin's overall conclusion that Mesklinites are, overall, not particularly alien. Still, what Martin and others see as Clement's artistic failing might be a necessary aspect of macrocosmic hard science fiction.

To explain the fact that the Mesklinites are so much like oceangoing merchants of Earth, one might observe that in creating worlds that humans can live on, and in creating worlds that are designed to serve as the settings for stories to be read by humans, writers of hard science fiction are governed by human priorities at all times—hence, the logic of making one's protagonists seem as human as possible.

As another explanation, one might recall C. S. Lewis's well-known response to the charge that science fiction generally pays little attention to character development: "It is absurd to condemn [science fiction stories] because they do not often display any deep or sensitive characterization .... Every good writer knows that the more unusual the scenes and events of his story are, the more ordinary, the more typical his persons should be. Hence Gulliver is a commonplace little man and Alice a commonplace little girl .... To tell how odd things struck odd people is to have an oddity too much" ("On Science Fiction" 64-65). Now, since the world of Mesklin is unquestionably "unusual" and "odd," it is only natural that Clement would want to make his protagonists seem as ordinary as possible, even though they are apparently very out of the ordinary; and in his discussion of *Mission of Gravity*, Gregory Benford specifically applies Lewis's argument to a defense of Clement's Mesklinites: "*Mission of Gravity* uses a gargantuan planet of crushing gravity; yet the aliens come over more like Midwesterners. (Maybe this was necessary at the time. The planet was so *outré*, Clement may have used ordinary aliens to keep things manageable.)" ("Effing the Ineffable" 16). Patricia Warrick, rising to the defense of another hard science fiction novel, James P. Hogan's *The Two Faces of Tomorrow*, makes a similar argument:

[H]ard science fiction is a literature so different from realistic fiction that the latter's critical standards are of limited use when evaluating hard science fiction. First, the scientist or engineer very often *is* a person lacking in the emotions and self-reflection upon which the drama of realistic fiction so often depends. The science fiction protagonist during the course of the novel discovers not some aspect of his own nature about which he was unaware, but rather some new aspect of the realm of knowledge. Science fiction is cerebral fiction, concerned with idea, not psychological fiction concerned with emotions and character development. ("Artificial Intelligence" 163)

However, there is another way to phrase Lewis's point that might rebut Martin's charge more effectively: When one observes a story apparently focused on characters that are rather drab and dull, one should first look around for other, more interesting characters that might be in the picture before condemning the author as negligent in that department. As observed in *A Fall of Moondust*, the trapped passengers, who would logically be regarded as the central characters, are in fact a rather uninteresting lot, but the people who work to rescue them turn out to be better developed and more rounded characters. In the case of *Mission of Gravity*, one could argue that the planet Mesklin is itself the main, and most interesting, character in the novel—an argument advanced by Donald M. Hassler, who called Mesklin "a fascinating character in its own right" (*Hal Clement* 22). In fact, Clement drops a rather large hint that Mesklin should be regarded this way in the first line of the novel: "The wind came across the bay like something living" (1). Natural wonders can be seen as living beings—and can be quite interesting if seen in that way. Thus, when Martin complains that "[T]he world overshadows its inhabitants," he is simply saying that the most interesting character in the novel overshadows its other characters; and Lewis's point could be restated as follows: that hard science fiction writers do not neglect characterization but rather will often apply their skills to characterizing objects that are not traditionally regarded as characters.

If a critic, then, decides to cast Mesklin as the protagonist of *Mission of Gravity*, there emerges another problem; despite its fascinating features, is the planet Mesklin in fact fully developed as a character? Here, I must confess what may be a personal failing in regard to the novel. At this time, I have attentively read *Mission of Gravity* four times and can count myself as someone reasonably familiar with the novel. However, when I recently reread the book I still found myself having difficulty in visualizing many aspects of Mesklin—its size, orbit, and the geography of Barlennan's journey. To get a better picture of Clement's creation, I turned to "Whirligig World," and there I found clear, well-organized explanations and diagrams that more or less explained the world in a satisfactory manner. However, even though *Mission of Gravity* does contain numerous passages of explanation, the novel itself somehow fails to convey much about the world of Mesklin very well.

One might explain this apparent problem by saying that Clement is not a very good writer—something Clement himself has repeatedly conceded, though perhaps with false modesty.[1] Yet if he could satisfactorily convey the characteristics of Mesklin in an article, he should have been able to do so in the novel as well. The difficulty, then, may be not a lack of talent but rather an ineffective writing strategy.

That is, there may also be something intrinsically problematic in writing about a place that is so vast and so different from traditional expectations; so special techniques are needed to introduce the new setting to readers. Larry Niven has spoken of his problems in writing *Ringworld*: "The difficult part was to describe [Ringworld] without losing the reader! This was an environment outside all common experience"; and Niven goes on to describe the various strategies he attempted:

I wanted the reader braced, forewarned against the Ringworld. I gave him the puppeteers' Fleet of Worlds as an intermediate step, to build his imagination. I showed him pictures and gave him scale comparisons and analogies. I stayed with one viewpoint and few characters, to keep it simple where I could. I let the size of the structure, the nature of it ("the mask of a world"), come as a recurring surprise to the characters. (introduction to an excerpt from *Ringworld* 122)[2]

But Clement employs no techniques like these; instead, he puts his readers on the planet Mesklin right away, on the first page of the novel. The question is: Why did Clement do it this way?

The answer, I believe, is that Clement developed as a writer during the 1940s, when John W. Campbell, Jr. became a dominant force in science fiction criticism by means of his editorship of *Astounding Science-Fiction*, his editorials on science fiction, and his introductions to various science fiction books. Campbell endorsed and repeatedly extolled the writings methods of Robert A. Heinlein, who began his stories in medias res and conveyed background information in casual asides; and Campbell once claimed that other approaches were rather old-fashioned:

[H. G.] Wells's method was to spend two chapters or so describing, for the reader, the cultural pattern he wanted to operate against. In the leisurely '90's and early twentieth century, that was permissible. The reader accepted it. Long descriptive passages were common. But the development of literary technique in the last third of a century has changed that; stage techniques, where long character-descriptions are ruled out, have moved into the novel field. To-day, a reader won't stand for pages of description of what the author thinks the character is like; let the character act, and show his character .... Heinlein was one of the first to develop techniques of story-telling that do it .... [A]n almost incredible mass of discussion somehow slipped in between without interrupting the flow of the action. ("Introduction," *The Man Who Sold the Moon* 14)

In fact, one can see *Mission of Gravity* as a conscious effort to emulate Heinlein's approach.[3] Clement begins the story well after the planet Mesklin has been discovered, after the Mesklinites had been contacted, and after the basic purpose of the mission had been established. He provides information about the planet and its inhabitants bit by bit in the first two pages: A reference to the "Rim of the World" is an early hint about the shape of the planet; the information that Barlennan's weight is "two and a quarter pounds instead of the five hundred and fifty or so to which he has been used all his life" suggests its variable gravity (1); a description of his crewmate's "six rearmost legs" (2) first evokes the unusual appearance of the Mesklinites; and the sudden revelation that the storm consisted of "droplets of methane" (2) indicates for the first time the unusual temperature and chemistry of the world. Also like Heinlein, Clement chooses characters who are already familiar with their environment, who can bring a certain sense of knowingness to their observations and actions; there is thus some logic beyond necessity in choosing a Mesklinite as his protagonist. Later on in the novel, there are more and more passages of explanation, and an attentive reader can presumably figure out everything that is going on; however, if I qualify as a typical reader, the process of doing so can be troublesome.

Particularly ineffective, I think, is the manner in which Clement conveys the unusual length of the Mesklinite day. In "Whirligig World," he simply comments that Mesklin "rotates on its axis at a trifle better than twenty degrees a minute, making the day some seventeen and three quarter minutes long" (108). But his novel is not so straightforward. The first use of the word—the Mesklinite sailors had stayed close to their ship "for the last ten days" (3)—gives no direct hint that the "day" in question is different from Earth's; neither does the next reference to a volcano that has "been spreading for days" (4). Soon afterward, however, comes the human's statement, "[Y]ou have thousands of days before you can get out" (4), an early indication that the "days" on Mesklin may be rather short. Other references—such as "in five or six thousand days" (6), "Land travel ... would not be fun for some thousands of days" (9), and "four hundred days passed before the storm let up" (11)—reinforce that suggestion.

The first statement that even indirectly specifies the length of the Mesklinite day is on page 22 of the original hardcover edition, when a human asks Barlennan if he started learning English less than six weeks ago and Barlennan replies, "I am not sure how long your 'week' is, but it is less than thirty-five hundred days" (21-22). At this point, an alert reader with a calculator can divide 42 Earthdays (6 weeks) by 3,500 Mesklindays to get a ratio of 0.012; multiplying that by 1,440 minutes, the number of minutes in an Earth-day, one can calculate the Mesklinite day as 17.28 minutes long, roughly Clement's figure. However, this does seem like rather a large amount of mental work for the alert reader. While other following references also suggest that the Mesklinite day is rather short, it is not until the end of Chapter 10—more than halfway through the novel—that Clement finally spells it out, announcing, "Sixty-five minutes" equals "rather less than four of Mesklin's days" (103). 65 minutes divided by 4—a much easier calculation—is 16.25 minutes, and since the 65 minutes are "rather less" than four Mesklinite days, one could with minimal effort estimate the length of the Mesklinite day as about 17, or a little more.

It is difficult to see, though, why Clement plays this guessing game with his readers. It would not have required "[l]ong descriptive passages" to specify the length of the Mesklinite day; a brief explanatory phrase would have sufficed. And since Clement throughout the novel employs the terms "hours" and "minutes" to refer to Earth's hours and minutes, it seems misleading to assign without explanation an entirely different meaning to the term *day*.

Although he does not apply the point specifically to this issue, Donald M. Hassler's *Hal Clement* offers grounds for a defense of Clement's approach in *Mission of Gravity*. According to Hassler, Clement is concerned with "issues of epistemology" and "suggests, in other words, that regardless of what symbol system we use to perceive and communicate we can never be sure exactly what the universe is made of .... [K]nowledge and the communication of knowledge are at best only partially efficient" (10,11). A parallel concern is language: "If partial knowledge is all we can hope to acquire, then, the perception of that knowledge and the communication of it through languages indicate both the limits of partiality and its only hope for accumulative gathering" (14).

From this perspective, Clement's use of the word *day* might be defended as an exercise illustrating the limitations of language and the possibility of overcoming those limitations. Humans now use the word *day* to mean two different things: (1) the length of time it takes a planet to finish a complete rotation (or the length of time it takes for its sun to return to its original position in that planet's sky) and (2) a fixed time period of approximately twenty-four hours. On Earth, the two meanings of *day* coincide, so there is no ambiguity. Once humans are imaginatively removed from the familiar environment of Earth and placed on a different planet, however, the crudeness of our language becomes a problem, because we are now in need of two different words, one to mean the period of a planet's rotation and one to mean twenty-four hours. In using the term on the planet Mesklin without any explanation, therefore, Clement reveals to his readers the limitations of their language: conditioned to think of a day as twenty-four hours, they fail to realize that its other natural meaning—a planet's period of rotation—allows a *day* to have an entirely different length. Still, by gradually learning more about this new world, and by applying that knowledge and their own intelligence to the problem, readers can eventually overcome this problem and recognize that a *day* on the planet Mesklin is significantly shorter than a day on Earth.

Ingenious as it is, this posited explanation strikes me as disingenuous. I reminded of a graduate seminar discussion of William Shakespeare's *King John*. After pointing out the obvious—that much of the play is boring—Professor Ricardo Quinones laughingly mentioned a critic who interpreted this boredom as Shakespeare's intent: To make a certain point, Shakespeare cleverly chose to write in a boring way. Indeed, almost any example of clumsiness or ineptitude in language might be defended as a deliberate authorial comment of some kind. I stand, then, by my objection that in describing the planet Mesklin, Clement is employing a technique that unnecessarily confuses the reader.[4]

I do not wish to belabor the problem with Clement's use of the word *day*; rather, I discuss it only as one illustration of a general difficulty: Clement's approach of dropping gradual hints leading up to eventual explanations, which worked so well in Heinlein's depictions of future societies on Earth, does not work as well in presenting an entirely alien environment; rather, it seems to demand too much alertness and mental activity from the readers. So there appears to be a need to return to something like "Wells's method" and begin at the beginning, slowly building up the imagined world with gradual and careful explanation. If *Ringworld* is taken as typical—and its approach is also seen in works like Clarke's *Rendezvous with Rama* and John Varley's *Titan*—then *Mission of Gravity* might be seen as a transitional novel: Clement has discovered the characteristic subject matter of macrocosmic hard science fiction, but has not discovered its characteristic writing technique.

One can readily imagine what *Mission of Gravity* would have been like if Clement had followed Niven's pattern. The novel would begin with the Earth explorers first discovering Mesklin, surveying the world, and deciding that it would in fact be an ideal place to employ a gravity probe. When the probe crashed, the men would land on the edge of the world—the only place where they could survive—to see if any kind of long-range rescue strategy might be used; and they would then discover the Mesklinites, tiny centipedelike creatures whose boats and artifacts testify to their intelligence. Gradually, they would teach the Mesklinites English and persuade them to undertake a mission to the fallen probe. This might have made for a duller beginning, and Clement may have been obliged to scramble to enliven the proceedings with dramatic incidents, but this approach would have thoroughly and clearly conveyed the world of Mesklin to readers.

In contrast, imagine what *Ringworld* would be like if Niven had followed Clement's approach. The story would begin with Louis Wu and his companions already on Ringworld and already familiar with its characteristics. As they trekked on, little asides and casual comments would gradually convey the information that they were in fact not on a normal world but on an immense, artificially constructed ring circling a star. Perhaps this would make for a more lively opening, but undoubtedly, readers of this novel would have had greater difficulty comprehending the nature of Ringworld.

Beyond his choice of introductory approach, there may be another explanation for Clement's apparent failure to completely convey the strangeness and enormity of his creation: One could argue that Clement simply does not feel capable of fully describing and conveying the enormity of his own creation and, hence, neglects the task. Even Niven himself still seems a little overwhelmed by his Ringworld: Introducing an excerpt, he says, "A quote that fully describes the Ringworld is impossible" (introduction 124). And Benford charges that, despite his careful efforts to introduce this construct, "Niven never quite brings home the colossal scale of his ringworld and the novel eventually turns into a catalog of spectacular pieces of landscape"—though he adds that "the imaginative thrust of the book is unquestioned" ("Science and Science Fiction" 32).

While I earlier dismissed a hypothetical defense of Clement's approach based on Hassler's analysis, I do not wish to dismiss Hassler's analysis; for the inherent limitations in knowledge-seeking and language are definitely one of Clement's concerns, and this concern is immediately relevant to the problems faced by the writer of macrocosmic hard science fiction. One might frame Clement's dilemma in writing *Mission of Gravity* in this way: The English language was developed, and has always been employed, to describe human beings and conditions on their home planet. Thus, when he attempts to depict beings very much unlike humans, the Mesklinites, and conditions very much unlike those on Earth, he finds that the language available to him is not up to the task. While this is a problem that, in a sense, virtually all science fiction writers sometimes face, it may be a special problem for writers of macrocosmic hard science fiction, since they have deliberately chosen as their subjects situations that are as different from the familiar as possible.

Here, the manner in which George Slusser's "Reflections on Style in Science Fiction" applies the work of Richard Ohmann to science fiction is relevant. As Slusser notes, Ohmann describes three types of "stylistic extrapolation" available to the science fiction writer—the uprooting of syntax, the neologism, and the metaphor (7-10)—which might be helpful in their attempt to depict their imaginative creations. None of these, however, seem particularly helpful to Clement's problem.

First, as he describes himself, Clement is not a masterful prose stylist, and it is difficult to imagine in any event how convoluted sentences and other stylistic experiments might have better conveyed the strangeness of Mesklin.

Second, some neologisms might have ameliorated some of his problems—for example, he might have started his novel using the term *Meskday* to immediately let readers know that this was not the ordinary Earth day—but large numbers of created terms, while they could serve to *suggest* the unusual nature of Mesklin, would not necessarily be effective in *describing* that unusual nature. And it is, in any event, a strategy that Clement rarely chooses to employ and does not seem comfortable with; when Darrell Schweitzer asked him "Did you ever feel inclined to design a future idiom for a story?" he responded, "Not to any great extent. I have sometimes invented a term or two which will apply to the situation, but if there is anything that is unpredictable, I'd say it would be slang" (Interview with Darrell Schweitzer 52).

Finally, Clement is aware of, and occasionally uses metaphors—as noted, the first sentence of *Mission of Gravity* likens a storm to a living being, and in his accompanying article, Mesklin was described as a "Whirligig"—but even extravagant metaphors could not fully convey all of the peculiar aspects of Mesklin.

Still, there is a fourth possible "stylistic extrapolation" available to Clement and other hard science fiction writers, although they almost never employ it in their writings, and that is the language of mathematics—formulas, equations, graphs, and diagrams. Clement, Anderson, Niven and others all tell their readers that their created worlds derive from mathematical formulas, the equations of Newton and his successors that exactly proscribe the nature and characteristics of large bodies in our universe. Presumably, it is by studying those equations and considering their implications that those writers come to a better understanding of their creations; indeed, one of the major uses of mathematics is to help people understand and manipulate objects beyond their experience. In human history, for example, there have only been a few people who could actually *visualize* four-dimensional objects, and two- and three-dimensional representations of those objects, which are kinds of visual metaphors, are only helpful to a limited extent. However, anyone familiar with mathematics can fully understand the equations that define four-dimensional objects and can reach substantive conclusions about their properties and characteristics.

Despite the apparent logic in doing so, though, only a very few writers of hard science fiction have ever incorporated equations into their stories—perhaps because they realize that the appearance of formulas and calculations would instantly alienate large numbers of their readers who are ignorant of, or uncomfortable with, mathematics.[5] One reason, then, that "Whirligig World" functioned as a better explanation of Mesklin was that it did include some charts, diagrams, and detailed discussions of the calculations Clement made. However, the overt use of mathematics in fiction, at this time, does not seem a realistic option for the hard science fiction writer: Even while addressing prospective science fiction writers in "The Creation of Imaginary Worlds," Anderson refrained from presenting equations, saying, "[T]oo many people are unreasonably puzzled, even frightened, by equations" (237). This remains, though, a theoretical possibility for hard science fiction, and one might imagine at some future time a new form of science fiction, aimed only at an extremely knowledgeable scientific audience, that would integrate imaginative language and imaginative mathematics, perhaps to convey posited new ideas and environments in a manner better than that of language alone or of mathematics alone.

As already suggested, the problem of describing a strange world like Mesklin is hardly unique to Clement or other hard science fiction writers; rather, it will always to some degree be a problem for all science fiction writers. However, writers of macrocosmic hard science fiction, in deliberately pushing themselves to imagine, develop, and describe the most unusual environments possible, face that problem to a much greater extent than writers who are simply imagining a space station, an inhabited moon base, or Earth as it will be fifty years in the future. In the final analysis, then, it may be unfair to criticize Clement because he is not capable of satisfactorily conveying his wonderful creation—in a sense, it is a *Mission* impossible.

There is one other way to characterize Clement's situation in writing *Mission of Gravity*—to see him not as an omniscient narrator, but as someone accompanying Barlennan on his journey, someone attempting to learn more about and better understand his own strange invention. It is significant, then, that one key theme of *Mission of Gravity* is, as Hassler has suggested, an ongoing quest for knowledge: When Barlennan asks his friend, "The knowledge that enables you to fly, then, cannot change weight?" he replies, "It cannot .... The instruments which are on that rocket grounded at your south pole should have readings that might teach us just that, in time .... We *must* have that data" (45). Hence, there may be three meanings in the novel's title: It is an important mission, a mission of gravity; it is a mission through an intense gravity field—a mission through gravity; and it is a mission to learn more about gravity—a mission about gravity.[6]

Overall, then, in macrocosmic hard science fiction, always mitigating that apparent inability to convey the bizarre and unprecedented is the opposing feeling that strange and wonderful novelties can "in time" be understood and mastered. This is not to say, as some imply, that hard science fiction writers all share a giddy, technophiliac optimism; rather, many writers seem well aware of the grievous problems that scientific progress may cause (see *A Fall of Moondust*) and well aware of the enormous difficulties involved in gaining new knowledge (see *Mission of Gravity*). However, as long as there is potentially useful work to be done, they are disinclined to surrender to passive pessimism regarding these challenges.

Still, there remains the possibility that this quest for knowledge will at some point reach a limit and become impossible to continue; what happens then? This is an issue raised by Charles Sheffield's *Between the Strokes of Night.*

NOTES

1. In "Ambivalence Towards 'Classes' or 'Genres': A Yoking of Anthony Trollope and Hal Clement," Hassler maintains that Clement tends to publicly dismiss his writing talents while privately harboring genuine literary aspirations—as seen, he argues, in the way that the titles to the chapters in his most recent novel, *Fossil*, form a perfect Shakespearean sonnet.

2. In reference to a related problem—conveying a vast expanse of time rather than space—Poul Anderson has also spoken of a special technique he used in writing *Tau Zero*, a novel involving a spaceship moving at ever faster relativistic speeds so that its passengers "outlived our cycle of the universe and saw a new cosmos reborn from the old." Seeking some way to convey such "enormousness," he studied the works of Olaf Stapledon and, finding that "His progression is logarithmic[,] I followed his lead. My first chapter covered a few hours, my second a few days, and so on, the period increasing by approximately a factor of ten in each successive chapter" ("Star-flights and Fantasies" 27-28). This "logarithmic" method to convey long periods of time—discussed in the next chapter—could also apply to introducing massive new worlds; and it is arguably the approach of *Ringworld*.

3. As evidence, one might also cite Clement's comment in "Hard Sciences and Tough Technologies" that "in science fiction, the background facts are less familiar to the reader and must be worked into the body of the story clearly, early, and unobtrusively" (42). The emphasis on facts "worked into" the story "unobtrusively" obviously reflects Clement's knowledge of Heinlein's technique, and of Campbell's espousal of that technique.

4. Still, I do regard Hassler's overall description of Clement's attitude as sound. The problem, though, is that once one accepts the limitations imposed by human language as a theme, an author might be tempted to be unambitious in her own use of language. Why bother struggling to achieve a perfectly descriptive and evocative prose style, since perfection in any expression of language is impossible? Indeed, Clement is certainly not incapable of writing effective prose—much of *The Nitrogen Fix* strikes me as unusually impressive in that area—but it sometimes seems that he is not really trying to write well. Certainly this is true of the most disappointing of Clement's recent novels, *Still River*.

5. One exception that comes to mind is Fred Hoyle's novel *The Black Cloud* (1957), even though the equations are carefully isolated in a footnote. A few other stories that include mathematical symbols and formulas are included in Clifton Fadiman's anthology *Fantasia Mathematica* (1958).

6. Hassler comments on the novel's title also capture these meanings: "*Mission of Gravity* is a grave and epic story with some very droll characters and situations—not exactly mock-epic, but definitely spaced-out epic and yet a very serious story about

journeying toward discovery" (*Hal Clement* 14). There is another possible meaning for the novel's title involving the old Latin word *gravitas*—dignity or decorum. The reason for the festering resentment Mesklinites feel towards humans that provokes the final crisis is not so much that the humans were withholding information from their alien cohorts, but that the humans *did not bother to explain why* they were withholding that information (their eventual explanation—that Mesklinites simply could not have comprehended most aspects of human science—satisfies Barlennan). In essence, the humans condescended to the Mesklinites, did not really talk to them as equals, did not treat them with proper dignity or decorum. Hence, one could argue, the novel is also a message about the importance of *gravitas*.

8

"Gazing Out at Infinity":
Charles Sheffield's *Between the*
Strokes of Night

There are any number of reasons why one might choose Charles Sheffield's *Between the Strokes of Night* as a final example of hard science fiction. First, like Arthur C. Clarke and Hal Clement, Sheffield is universally accepted as a hard science fiction writer: The back cover of *Between the Strokes of Night* includes review quotations describing him as "a master of the hard science story," announcing that "Sheffield's name has become synonymous with intriguing 'hard' science fiction," and calling his works "the best modern examples of 'hard' science fiction." As another indication of his close connection to hard science fiction, *Between the Strokes of Night* makes specific references to Sheffield's two most distinguished predecessors in the field, Clarke and Clement. The novel quotes Clarke's statement, "Any sufficiently advanced technology is indistinguishable from magic," though it is coyly attributed to "pre-Flight philosopher/writer Isaac (?) Clarke" (121), and one planet his characters visit, called Whirligig, recalls Clement's "Whirligig World" and in fact is a younger version of Mesklin, a world that has only had a rapid spin for about 100,000 years and hence is only slightly oblate.

In addition, *Between the Strokes of Night* can represent what I have previously called the combined form of hard science fiction, beginning as microcosmic hard science fiction, then abruptly shifting into macrocosmic hard science fiction; and the novel, in ultimately moving billions of years into the future, also represents the form of macrocosmic hard science fiction that, like Poul Anderson's *Tau Zero*, presents a vast expanse of time, rather than a vast expanse of space. Its two major parts can provoke a discussion of two common forms of modern hard science fiction that might be referred to as the space frontier novel and the juvenile novel. Finally, I happen to believe it is an important and neglected novel which is not necessarily out of place in a discussion that includes *A Fall of Moondust* and *Mission of Gravity*.

The first part of the novel is set in the near future and focuses on a scientific research project, designed to lengthen the human life span, that moves from New Zealand to a space station while Earth reels from one devastating crisis to another. This section basically follows a common pattern in recent novels about near-future space travel, that I call the space frontier novel. These works typically build on a number of assumptions:

1. Earth in the near future will continue to be beset by a host of problems, including overpopulation; various forms of air, water, and land pollution; shortages of food, energy, and mineral resources; drought and other disastrous climatic changes; terrorism and political instability; and the threat of massive nuclear, biological, or chemical warfare.

2. Although the cause of most of these problems is technological, the posited solution is more technology: most typically, a massive investment in space travel and space colonies—that will provide unlimited energy, resources, and wealth—although other types of ambitious research projects may also be seen as part of the solution.

3. Unfortunately, the short-sighted, petty-minded bureaucrats of Earth governments will stubbornly refuse to see the wisdom of space activities. Instead, they will repeatedly move to limit, restrict, or even cancel existing space initiatives.

4. Thus, it will be left to energetic individualists—such as visionary billionaires or renegade astronauts—to move forcefully into space and exploit its vast resources.

5. Their efforts will be vigorously resisted by Earth's decadent bureaucracies, that will resort to everything from economic restrictions to all-out war in an effort to control or eliminate the space pioneers.

6. Ultimately, the space pioneers will prove victorious, and they will progress onward to greater success and prosperity, while the people of Earth sink further into poverty, decadence, or even extinction.

Norman Spinrad aptly summarized the attitudes in such stories:

The asteroids (colonial America or the Old West) were seen as the free frontier, the future of economic (and sometimes political) freedom, colonized by rugged individualists who were usually fighting for economic and/or political independence from wicked, degenerate, collectivist, played-out Earth (old Europe or the effete East). Out there in the Belt, with its limitless mineral resources, its low gravity and its wide-open spaces, was the future of the species, and as for poor old polluted, overpopulated screwed-up Earth, well, tough shit .... Not all of this stuff had a right-wing political message, and not all of it limited the frontier to the Asteroid Belt, but all of it displayed much of the same attitude towards Earth and what it stood for. Poor old Earth was unsalvageable and at best must be left to stew in its own juices while the best and the brightest headed in the direction of Pluto. ("Dreams of Space" 127)

In the case of *Between the Strokes of Night*, the problems on Earth are most prominently famine, climatic change, and worldwide political tension; the posited solutions are not only more investment in space but also a project to prolong human life and reduce the need for sleep; the bureaucrats are resisting continued support for this research; the visionary individualist is billionaire Salter Wherry, who starts constructing several massive space habitats for people to inhabit and travel to other solar systems in; he is resented and resisted by the governments of Earth, though they cannot restrain him; and after Wherry persuades the sleep researchers to accept his generous support and relocate to his space station, the entire human population of Earth is quickly wiped out by a global nuclear war.

There are two general comments to make about this sort of story. First, there is no particular reason to see such scenarios as a necessary result of writing hard science fiction. True, many writers connected to the subgenre, like Ben Bova, Jerry Pournelle, and Larry Niven, have written stories in this vein; but a number of other hard science fiction writers, including Clarke, Clement, and Gregory Benford, have never written anything like them. On the other hand, there have been space frontier novels written by people like Melisa Michaels (*First Battle*) and Dana Stabenow (*Second Star*) whose knowledge of science seems superficial and derivative and who therefore cannot be properly considered hard science fiction writers. The space frontier novel, therefore, is a form of writing that often intersects with hard science fiction, but it should not be identified with it.

Second, those hard science fiction novels which fit the pattern of the space frontier novel, like Ben Bova's *Millennium* or Larry Niven and Jerry Pournelle's "Spirals," demonstrate even more clearly than *A Fall of Moondust* or *Mission of Gravity* that the supposedly objective process of writing hard science fiction is in fact strongly infused with a commitment to human values. In producing these stories, writers do not carefully and unemotionally extrapolate scientific facts toward new and unsettling realizations; instead, they ruthlessly twist scientific facts to make their future worlds conform to ancient and comfortable patterns. Space literally becomes the New American West in stories like Katherine MacLean's "The Gambling Hell and the Sinful Girl," the story of a simple girl from the Ozarks who samples the corruption of big-city life directly transplanted to the asteroid belt; and novels like Robert A. Heinlein's *The Moon Is a Harsh Mistress*—the *ur*-text from that so many later works of this type derive—blatantly retell the story of the American Revolution, with the moon or a space habitat representing America and the Earth representing England.

While other Sheffield stories, like *The McAndrew Chronicles*, seem strongly influenced by the space frontier novel, Sheffield clearly wishes to disassociate *Between the Strokes of Night* from this type of writing. Accordingly, the book has little, if any, rhetoric about the necessity for space travel, the superiority of life in space, or the need for clear-thinking individuals to struggle against the stupid bureaucrats. And far from expressing contempt for the people of Earth, his characters express genuine compassion for their plight: "The explosions went on and on, in a ghastly silence of display that almost seemed worse than any noise. Did she wish the screen showed an image of North America? Or would she rather not know what had happened there? With all her relatives in Chicago and Washington, there seemed no hope for any of them" (106).[1]

In addition, Sheffield lets readers know right away that his novel has broader concerns than simply promoting space activities by beginning *Between the Strokes of Night* with a brief Prologue written in the far future by one of his characters. And there is one moment in the first part of the novel that perfectly foreshadows the theme of the novel: One of the sleep researchers, after first boarding the space station, "made his way to the outermost corridor of Spindletop, where the effective gravity was highest, and a quarter-gee was almost enough to bring his stomach in line; but if he allowed himself to look down, he was gazing *out* at infinity, standing on a rotating sea of stars that swirled steadily beneath his feet. And that was enough to start him off again" (88). In fact, "gazing out at infinity" will become the major impetus guiding these characters' behavior.

After Earth is destroyed, and the director of the sleep research appears ready to become the first person to experience a longer life span, the novel abruptly shifts 25,000 years into the future, to begin what seems like an entirely new story. On the planet Pentecost, some superior young people are competing in the Planetfest, a grueling series of physical and mental challenges; the winners will get to travel into space, meet the mysterious Immortals who seem to dominate life on their planet, and—perhaps—get to unravel some of the mysteries involving the Immortals and the fate of previous Planetfest winners. Along with these shifts of time, place and characters, there is a shift of genre too, for in focusing on the thoughts and experiences of several young people, *Between the Strokes of Night* now takes on the trappings of a juvenile novel.

As mentioned earlier, the nascent genre of juvenile science fiction showed an immediate affinity for hard science fiction in the 1950s, as represented by numerous stories about travelling into space, building space stations, and colonizing the moon and Mars. Many prominent hard science fiction writers, including Poul Anderson, Clarke, Clement, Benford, and Bova, have produced books that were labelled juvenile science fiction; while another novel by Clement, *Cycle of Fire*, was initially marketed as an adult novel but later successfully repackaged as a juvenile, suggesting that other hard science fiction books could be similarly regarded as true juveniles.

Indeed, it could be maintained that hard science fiction—particularly its macrocosmic variety—is an approach particularly well suited for stories written for a juvenile audience. For one thing, as suggested by the analysis of *Mission of Gravity*, macroscopic hard science fiction novels may invariably focus more on their scientific creations than on their characters, and juvenile science fiction is traditionally inhabited by flat and superficial characters. In addition, the juvenile science fiction novel is typically a story about education, and this format allows for numerous educational lectures to be delivered by adults to young-sters—a perfect format for the scientific explanations that are often necessary to stories of this type. More broadly, the juvenile science fiction novel is about progressing from ignorance to knowledge, from powerlessness to power, and one can argue that this is the characteristic story of science itself and the characteristic narrative structure of both forms of hard science fiction.

All of these features surface in the second part of *Between the Strokes of Night*. While Sheffield's young people may be better drawn than most in labeled juvenile fiction, they remain not so much characters as types—questing young people searching for answers and a purpose in life. The mysteries they confront—who are the Immortals? Are they really immortal, and can they really travel faster than light? And what is the reason for their strange behavior?—overshadow any concern for their development as characters. When they travel into space and meet the Immortals, large undiluted amounts of exposition and explanation are worked into their conversations with these adult figures. And having finally reached the true headquarters of the Immortals, the young people are then accepted as Immortals themselves, and they become prime movers in the ongoing quest to understand more about the universe.

One might, with a modicum of justice, classify many works of hard science fiction as a form of juvenile literature,[2] and this might become the basis for a defense against the standard charge, raised by Sheffield and noted earlier, that "the hard SF label carries with it the stigma ... of poor characterization, tin ears, and a lack of sensitivity to everything that cannot be assigned a number" (Letter 4). That is, one should not necessarily expect literary quality in a story aimed primarily at younger readers. Thomas M. Disch, who often argues that science fiction in general might be best considered juvenile literature, has specifically applied this argument to one of the stories frequently associated with hard science fiction, Tom Godwin's "The Cold Equations": "As a specimen of English prose, of character portrayal, of sociological imagination, the story can only be judged as puerile; yet within its own terms, as a fable designed to convey to very young people that science is not a respecter of persons, it is modestly successful" ("The Embarrassments of Science Fiction" 143).

Sheffield's shift into juvenile science fiction also has broader implications involving the two forms of hard science fiction I have identified. Indeed, the fact that the two parts of his novel involve such different approaches suggests another key element in the distinction between those forms.

Microcosmic hard science fiction, featuring imagined new devices of the near future, naturally lends itself to stories of the scientist as hero, to a focus on the person creating or supervising the new technology. This is certainly true of Clarke's *A Fall of Moondust*, where the main heroes are the astronomer who locates the missing craft and the engineer who rescues its passengers. Like the first part of *Between the Strokes of Night*, it is a story about powerful people, mastering a new aspect of science.

The second half of Sheffield's novel, however, like other stories of juvenile science fiction, is a story of less-than-powerful people, youngsters who must try to figure out or overcome the power structure imposed and governed by adults. And while developing his new young protagonists, Sheffield interestingly recharacterizes the protagonists of the first part of the novel. It is curious to note how the scientists studying longevity, initially cast as the novel's heroes, later take on the role of villains, manipulating young people without informing them about what is really going on, seeking to imprison them when they overstep their boundaries, and generally functioning as distant and mysterious overlords. Even though one of the young people in *Between the Strokes of Night* is ultimately invited to become part of the team, the characters that the readers were initially asked to identify with remain oddly unsympathetic.

This change from adult to juvenile fiction, from manipulating heroes to manipulated heroes, can be seen as a consequence of the change from microcosmic to macrocosmic hard science fiction. In the former, the scientific advances and machinery are small matters, easy to depict as under the control of smoothly competent heroes. In the latter, however, the new scientific element literally expands to cosmic size, to become not a new spaceship or machine but an entire new world. Such a vast and strange new environment cannot readily be envisioned as something controlled by any people that readers can identify with. There are then two possible ways to change the story in response to this shift in scale: First, the people seen as in charge of the creation might become correspondingly more powerful and less human, and hence less effective as heroes, requiring a new focus on other, less powerful people as the protagonists, the strategy observed in *Between the Strokes of Night*.[3] A second approach would be to eliminate altogether the role of people as masters, picturing the vast new world as something created by God, nature, or invisible artisans, and again providing the story with weaker heroes whose task is to explore and puzzle out the world—the strategy observed in Niven's *Ringworld*, John Varley's *Titan*, and other works about huge and awesome new environments.

Of course, all the amazing new worlds of macrocosmic hard science fiction are in fact created and controlled by one very human figure—the author—that suggests yet another way to characterize the peculiar tensions in that form. I earlier suggested that the planet Mesklin itself might be seen as the protagonist of *Mission of Gravity*; but one could also argue that *Clement* is the hero of the story, the one person who developed and fully understands the intriguing environment that is displayed. In microcosmic hard science fiction, the small scale of the imagined scientific discovery allows for a focus on powerful but recognizably human protagonists; in macrocosmic hard science fiction, the characters are dwarfed by the created environment, making them seem like juveniles in spirit if not in depicted chronological age, and the author-as-unseen-God comes to function as the dominant character. In the case of *Between the Strokes of Night*, it is a vast increase in the scale of the human life span, and a corresponding increase in one's perceptions of the universe, that is Sheffield's creation; the characters seen as controlling this newly lengthened humanity seem cold and distant; the characters we can identify with seem almost helpless—even though they do achieve a small victory of sorts over their long-lived superiors; and it is admiration for Sheffield's vision, rather than concern for either set of characters, that ultimately dominates the reader's response to the novel.

It is odd, then, that a form of writing united by an obsessive concern for scientific rigor should be so radically transformed by a simple change in scale. Dealing with cautious predictions of near-future scientific advances, writers naturally accept the notion that scientific progress should be shaped by human values, resulting in stories that satisfyingly reflect human concerns and emotions. Moving into the creation of bizarre new worlds and vast expanses of space and time, writers are driven to an attitude that casts human values as unimportant, as the author and the created environment become the focus of attention and the characters seem either distant and inhuman, like the Immortals of *Between the Strokes of Night*, or weak and flat, like Sheffield's contestants or the Mesklinites who so much resemble European sailors in Clement's *Mission of Gravity*. What the two forms of hard science fiction have in common, besides their concern for science, is the limitation imposed by human perspectives: In microcosmic hard science fiction, writers embrace and celebrate that limitation; in macrocosmic hard science fiction, writers seem to butt their heads in frustration against those limitations.

Having previously examined how Clement and Niven are ultimately unsuccessful in truly evoking their vast creations, I must now address Sheffield's attempt to convey an awe-inspiring vision of a huge and endless universe, the subject of the final section of *Between the Strokes of Night*. In one sense, Sheffield here confronts a portentous issue that has bothered many other science fiction writers: The universe seems far too large in comparison with a human, so how it is possible for people to conquer, or even comprehend, the universe? One common answer to this question, found in works like Olaf Stapledon's *Star Maker*, Arthur C. Clarke's *Childhood's End*, and George Zebrowski's *Macrolife*, is to imagine humans, or humans and aliens, coming together to form one massive group-mind—thus transforming themselves into a single being that is both huge and immortal—but this solution can seem unpalatable because it implies the loss of the individual conscience.[4] Sheffield offers a simpler and possibly more satisfying answer: If humans could only live longer—much longer, on a scale of millions or years instead of years—they would indeed have enough time to study and understand the universe.

There are two solutions of this type offered in the novel. First, humans may live in "S-Space," a newly discovered, slower metabolic state where a normal human year might seem like only a day. This is the realm where the Immortals live, and, coupled with other techniques for extending one's perceived life span to 1700 years, living in S-Space gives humans an effective life span of millions of years. Second, as revealed in the last part of the novel, there is another, even slower metabolic state available—"T-Space"—where one might live billions of years. And it is in this state that one winner of the Planetfest, Sy Day, ultimately elects to spend his days, so that he can, in the last scene of the novel, witness the final collapse, and possible rebirth, of the universe billions of years in the future.

There is a problem with these new states of life, however. In S-Space, the contestants find, colors look dimmer, food tastes blander, and sexual activity is less pleasurable. In general, everyday life in S-Space lacks spice and flavor, and it also seems that human thinking and creativity are limited in this state; it is only by going in normal space that innovative solutions to problems can be found. Thus, one climax of the novel comes when Wolfgang Gibbs, a character who previously lived in S-Space, elects to go back to N-Space, or normal space, to live a brief but more productive life.

In a way, then, this novel confronts more honestly the dilemma of Tom Godwin's "The Cold Equations"—the dichotomy between human aspirations and the reality of the universe—but avoids the pat answer that the universe simply represents the negation of human values. Rather, its answer is more complex: Humans can become more like the universe in their life span and perceptions and thus better deal with the reality of the universe; however, this does mean they will have to lose part of their humanity—although they do not exactly become unfeeling robots. Yes, the universe is not amenable to purely human wishes, but it is not totally inhuman either.

Still, one can question the genuine novelty or logic of the new states of existence that Sheffield describes. Some aspects of their new life—such as the paleness of the light they see and the lack of taste in the food—could be regarded as deductions based on scientific data, since people moving at a slower rate of speed would perceive light at different wavelengths and, being colder as well, might have trouble tasting certain spices. The concept that such beings would feel generally listless and unimaginative, however, does not seem supported by scientific reasoning; rather, it appears to derive from the common and well-established nexus of meanings associated with the word *slow*. Arguably, people living at lower temperatures might feel somewhat invigorated—after all, this is what many people who live in cold climates report—and people living at a slower rate of speed might be better and more creative thinkers, having the ability to reason matters out carefully and thoroughly rather than at the forced rapidity of normal human existence. One must wonder, then, whether Sheffield has really achieved a truly scientific understanding of the possibilities in the kind of existence he imagines, or whether he is instead falling back on preconceptions derived from human language and traditions.

Between the Strokes of Night also appears to have difficulty grappling with the other great mystery it presents: the apparent existence of other life forms—small beings called Gossameres and Pipistrelles, and larger Kermel Objects—that inhabit the spaces between stars and galaxies. The humans who study the Kermel

Objects can only determine that they are intelligent and that they are sending messages to each other; but their origins and motives are otherwise unknown.

At this point, Sheffield's novel seems to end abruptly. While one might expect, following this revelation, that the novel would proceed to describe how humans in S-Space and T-Space went on to learn more about the Kermel Objects, and even contact them, Sheffield instead offers a brief coda, set billions of years in the future, when the universe is coming to an end. Sy Day, who chose to remain in T-Space, is there to observe everything in the universe, including the still-mysterious Kermel Objects, converging toward a single point in a reversal of the process that began the universe. Despite what we must presume are billions of years of research, unanswered questions remain in Sy's mind: "[S]cience and logic tell me to expect [that] at the final mini-microsecond, in the terminal instant of un-creation, everything disintegrates .... unless, perhaps, consciousness can transcend the limitations of physics? I do not know. Less than one minute from the end, the nature of reality still eludes me." All Sy can do is "proclaim" his "faith": *"I have made no error. I have interpreted the message of the Kermel Objects correctly. The end is the beginning. There will be tomorrow"* (346).

To some, it might seem strange that a hard science fiction novel would end with a proclamation of "faith"—but in a sense, it is not so unusual. All science is, as Louise B. Young has noted, based on "the assumption that is common to all scientific thought: there is an order in nature that can be understood by the human mind .... the *faith* that there is some kind of common denominator in the apparent diversity of nature has not wavered" ("Mind and Order in the Universe" 445-446; my italics). Confronted with questions that remain unresolved, the scientist cannot accept that they are unresolvable; always there is the belief that someone, someday, will be able to figure them out. Thus, the "faith" that Sy finally proclaims is nothing more or less than the faith that sustains science itself.

Of course, a hard science fiction novel that ends by offering *faith* instead of firm projections is also not very different than other science fiction novels—that suggests a tentative conclusion: Writers of hard science fiction might indeed have a special skill for creating and approaching concepts that are truly inhuman or alien; but their scientific knowledge and training are not particularly helpful in developing and fully realizing these concepts. Reaching the threshold of the truly unknown, hard science fiction writers, like other science fiction writers, may find themselves forced to rely on metaphor, common sense, and intuition—that is, they may be forced back on purely human, rather than scientific, systems of thought.[5]

There is a possible connection between this final recourse to scientific faith and the mood that is often attributed to many macrocosmic hard science fiction novels—a feeling of *transcendence* and religious awe. Clement and Niven keep their attitudes fairly down-to-Earth, but other writers like Clarke and Gregory Benford freely surrender to this atmosphere when they are depicting their grandest creations. As noted, P. Schuyler Miller referred to this mood when speaking of the "poetic" Clarke, while Algis Budrys spoke of certain Clarke works as "mystical."

Here, we may be dealing with some programming that is part of human nature, even though it is not necessarily reasonable. Logically, there is no reason to connect huge objects and grand visions with the Almighty; logically, one can see the work of God in a geranium as well as the Grand Canyon. Nevertheless, it seems a normal human reaction to be awestruck by visions of enormity. C. S. Lewis noted this attribute in H. G. Wells's *The Time Machine*, Olaf Stapledon's *Last and First Men*, and Clarke's *Childhood's End*, works that he describes as "Eschatological": "It is sobering and cathartic to remember, now and then, our collective smallness, our apparent isolation, the apparent indifference of nature, the slow biological, geological, and astronomical processes that may, in the long run, makes many of our hopes (possibly some of our fears) ridiculous" ("On Science Fiction" 66). And in his interview with Jeffrey M. Elliot, Gregory Benford has argued that a similar impulse toward awe and grandiosity is one of the main attractions of science fiction in general, and of hard science fiction in particular:

[E]verything astronomical is literally astronomical; it has an immense impact on people. One of the discoveries that has come out of the last century, it seems to me, is that we live in a very comfortable pocket of the universe, for that we've been designed, not the other way around. This is very apparent once you get out above the thin skin of the atmosphere. Science fiction brings this truth to the fore .... It's this ability to get longer perspectives, to get wider scopes, that attracts people to science fiction, particularly the astronomical kind of science fiction. Usually, this means the "hard" kind of science fiction—namely, rocket ships, strange planets, etc. That's one reason, though, that most of the prominent science fiction writers write "hard" science fiction. (Interview with Jeffrey M. Elliot 47)

More recently, Benford has suggested that this mood is a key characteristic of hard science fiction: "[T]he often-invoked emotions behind much hard SF—awe and thinly veiled transcendence .... are the core passions of Clarke and Stapledon" ("Time and *Timescape*" 190).

In the case of *Between the Strokes of Night*, all of these concerns are clearly at the forefront. Indeed, one could plausibly offer C. S. Lewis's statement—"our collective smallness, our apparent isolation, the apparent indifference of nature, the slow biological, geological, and astronomical processes that may, in the long run, makes many of our hopes (possibly some of our fears) ridiculous"—as the central message of the novel. Thus, the impulse towards religious feelings in macrocosmic hard science fiction—that seems on the surface a tendency directly counter to the scientific bent of its creators—may only reflect the fact that these stories often create huge things, or deal with huge amounts of time, and that human beings typically react to huge things with a sense of awe and reverence, even the human beings that created them.

In attempting to evoke vast expanses of time and space, *Between the Strokes of Night* finally seems to exhibit the same problem Clement confronted in *Mission of Gravity*: the limitations of human language. Here, writers have the advantage of numerical terms, but one can question whether these are really sufficient: Does the phrase "four billion years" really convey exactly how long such a period of time would be? Certainly, in a language where a "long life" might be one hundred years, there is no truly effective vocabulary for describing billions of years—or billions of light-years, for that matter. In the context of the rest of the novel, the coda to *Between the Strokes of Night* might be seen as breathtakingly short and unevocative; and yet, that conclusion may also be the novel's greatest virtue.

Arguably, efforts in science fiction to evoke a truly cosmic vision have been largely unsuccessful—understandably so, given the immense difficulty of the task. One could of course mention Stapledon's *Star Maker*, but even that impressive novel seems to grow diffuse and metaphorical in its final attempt to present a multitude of universes; other, lesser novels, like Zebrowski's *Macrolife*, noticeably falter in their expansive conclusions. The apparently inappropriate brevity and crypticness of Sheffield's coda, then, might be read as an authorial statement: As my characters and narrative grow beyond a purely human perspective, a human author like myself can no longer describe them properly; hence, I will not even make the effort. Sheffield's purpose, like Clement's, may be to explore and reveal the fundamental limitations of human language and perception; and readers who initially feel disappointed by the abrupt conclusion of *Between the Strokes of Night* may realize, on reflection, that their sense of disappointment conveys the true enormity and mystery of the universe in a manner far more effective than grandiose imagery or clever wordplay.[6]

Hard science fiction, it seems, can confront the fundamental issue of limited human wishes versus unlimited natural realities—but it does not manifest any special ability to resolve such issues and indeed might make that very inability into its major theme. Like other types of fiction, hard science fiction typically becomes uncertain and tentative at the crucial eschatological moment. Thus, while hard science fiction might arguably be an unusually effective way of "gazing out at infinity," even hard science fiction writers may have trouble making sense out of what they see.

One may take *Between the Strokes of Night*, then, as an illustrative model of the powers and the limitations of hard science fiction. In his first two sections, Sheffield shows what hard science fiction can do well—realistic portrayals of near-future possibilities, and vast new environments created by scientific thinking; and in his short final section, Sheffield shows what hard science fiction cannot do well—describe what is truly vast beyond comprehension, what is truly inhuman or alien.

To summarize my discussions of *A Fall of Moondust*, *Mission of Gravity*, and *Between the Strokes of Night*: Despite the emphasis on machinery in microcosmic hard science fiction, and despite the strangeness and immensity of the creations in macrocosmic hard science fiction, both forms are driven to focus on solving human problems and providing a limited human perspective. Indeed, the focus on scientific data and thinking may inexorably evoke a human response, making descriptions of hard science fiction as "cold" or "inhuman" basically inaccurate. Coldness and inhumanity do enter science fiction, but perhaps, as already suggested, forms of science fiction other than hard science fiction most naturally give rise to this mood.

What all three examples of the form examined here suggest is that hard science fiction is—as John J. Pierce has said, but for different reasons (as discussed below)—"a quite limited literary form" ("The Literary Experience of Hard Science Fiction" 182). Its limits are self-imposed by the author and, as Gregory Benford indicates in "Is There a Technological Fix for the Human Condition?" those limits may provide a tremendous stimulus for imaginative creation; however, those limits may also inhibit the process of imaginative creation in some ways. On the basis of its novelty or literary value, then, it seems difficult to argue that hard science fiction represents either the pinnacle or the nadir of science fiction writing; for some of its works stand among the most noteworthy achievements in the genre, while others are dull and mediocre. As with all science fiction, it appears, aesthetic evaluation of hard science fiction must proceed on a case-by-case basis; in the words of Poul Anderson, "Whether a work is 'hard' or 'soft' has nothing whatsoever to do with its literary merit *per se*" (Interview with Jeffrey M. Elliot 43).

One might turn at this point to Pierce's argument in "The Literary Experience of Hard Science Fiction"—that the characteristic impulse of hard science fiction is simply to create new realities—not new metaphors—and hence that its various purposes are at odds with traditional literary goals.[7] From this perspective, the value of *A Fall of Moondust* is that it envisions an entirely new form of transportation and an entirely new type of human disaster; the value of *Mission of Gravity* is that it envisions a new and different type of habitable planet and environment; and the value of *Between the Strokes of Night* is that it envisions a radically transformed type of humanity that might endure to witness the end of the universe. Yet much of what I suggest here works to undermine this defense. After all, if the near-future extrapolations of microcosmic hard science fiction are governed by a desire to make scientific realities conform to human needs and expectations, and if the imaginative creations of macrocosmic hard science fiction are restrained by the limits of human language and imagination, then just how new can the new realities of this subgenre be?[8] In Pierce's view, then, hard science fiction is limited because its authors are not interested in traditional literary goals; I am driven to conclude that the form is limited because the authors themselves are limited in their pursuit of untraditional goals.

Overall, hard science fiction seems to represent an unconventional *method* of writing science fiction that does not necessarily create unconventional stories. It is an answer, I suspect, that will please no one on either side of the hard science fiction debate.

NOTES

1. One could argue, in fact, that the entire first part of the novel takes its shape solely as a way to prepare for the rest of Sheffield's story. That is, in order to establish a race of life-extended humans, he must first explain the research that led to that condition, and in order to explain why such beings could come to dominate human civilization, he must first destroy the planet Earth.

2. This is not necessarily a criticism, as I discuss in "The Genre That Evolved: On Science Fiction as Children's Literature."

3. I am reminded here of the strange woman who governs—or who in a sense *is*—the artificial world in John Varley's *Titan*, who remains unseen throughout most of the novel; even though a final scene attempts to make her seem normal and approachable, she remains distant and enigmatic.

4. However, another novel on this theme—Spider and Jeanne Robinson's *Stardance*—specifically addresses this issue and has its transformed characters explicitly argue, not altogether convincingly, that their participation in the group-mind is only an accompaniment to, not a replacement of, their individual consciousnesses.

5. The novel to mention here may be Poul Anderson's *Tau Zero*, which graphically describes how a spaceship is incredibly accelerated so that its passengers' lives are slowed down to the point that they can advance billions of years and witness the end of the universe—yet they ultimately become preoccupied with their own personal situations instead of the grandeur and mystery of what they witness.

6. This argument, of course, is vulnerable to the sort of objection I early anticipated: that I am attempting to excuse a flawed passage by maintaining that the author deliberately wrote in a flawed manner. Still, given Sheffield's demonstrated talents, and given that there are any number of obvious ways he might have worked to expand or amplify his conclusion, it is at least somewhat plausible to maintain that the brevity and inadequacy of his final section represent a deliberate decision.

7. As Pierce acknowledges, this position can be derived from the critical writings of Samuel R. Delany.

8. In addition, this defense of hard science fiction cannot be restricted to hard science fiction because, as previously suggested, some of the most impressive and imaginative creations in science fiction—such as Olaf Stapledon's cosmic visions, Ursula K. Le Guin's Gethenians, and William Gibson's cyberspace—have come from writers who have not been strongly associated with hard science fiction.

9

Conclusion

On one side stand the advocates of hard science fiction, dedicated to cold, objective scientific reality and the denial of outmoded humanistic aspirations. On the other side stand the advocates of soft science fiction, dedicated to a reaffirmation of those traditional aspirations. These implacably opposed factions struggle to seize control of the "center" of science fiction.

This is not literary criticism; this is mythology.

It is mythology founded, as I have argued, on a misunderstanding regarding the term's etymology and on an outdated and inaccurate view of modern scientific reality. It is mythology that ignores the fact that virtually all writers of science fiction agree on the importance of adhering to the laws of science—they differ not in kind but only in the degree to which they will indulge in gobbledygook or "fudging" to avoid scientific errors. It is mythology which fails to note that only a small handful of writers have ever been regularly labelled hard science fiction writers, and that there has never been a recognized category of *soft science fiction*, nor anyone who has stepped forward to advocate that form.

There may be some value in painting science fiction in broad strokes, establishing principles that divide the field into all-embracing categories for the purpose of critical examination.[1] As I have attempted to show, though, using *hard science fiction* as one label in such dichotomies is an abuse of the term. Indeed, one benefit of my research is to provide some grounds for placing reasonable limitations on the meaning of the term.

In "On *The True History of Science Fiction*" and elsewhere, I have argued that a study of the critical commentaries surrounding modern science fiction constitutes the best starting point for studies of the genre; I argue here, as one conclusion of my work, that the same is true of hard science fiction. The term cannot be allowed to mean whatever a given critic wants it to mean; and to challenge, for example, Michael Collings's characterization of C. S. Lewis as a hard science fiction writer (in "Science and Scientism in C. S. Lewis's *That Hideous Strength*"), one may not be convincing in saying, "In my opinion, he is not a hard science fiction writer," since Collings can reply, "In my opinion, he is." Knowing the critical history of hard science fiction, however, one can say, "Lewis is not a hard science fiction writer for these reasons: In the first twenty years when the term was regularly employed, he was never called a hard science fiction writer, even by commentators like Miller who were well aware of his work; Lewis's novels do not fulfill all traits usually announced as characteristic of the form, such as extreme attentiveness to scientific fact and scientific extrapolation—in fact, Lewis at more than one time announced his complete indifference toward scientific accuracy;[2] and in his own remarks on hard science fiction (which he called *Engineers' Stories*) Lewis expressed disdain for the form, further distancing himself from it." Because I can bring forth an entire body of critical commentary, and not just my own theoretical constructs, to defend my opinions, that constitutes, I submit, a more powerful rebuttal.

It is also worth noting that many hard science fiction writers like Charles Sheffield have, as noted, argued for a rather narrow interpretation of the term. And the metaphor for the subgenre Sheffield employs—the limerick—further implies that hard science fiction is a minor, almost trivial subgenre of science fiction; that is, the same analogy might have been made using some form of poetry that is more common and more respected, like Gregory Benford's sonnet. In Sheffield's view, then, hard science fiction is a rare and peculiar obsession in science fiction, comparable to the limerick in poetry—and is not one of two broad categories encompassing the entire field.

If critics therefore eschew all efforts to expand the subgenre beyond tradition or reason, and focus instead on "the generally accepted meaning" of hard science fiction, as defined by its texts and commentaries, one result is that it becomes possible to develop a description of the subgenre.[3] Some may feel, true, that a description of this kind is by nature impossible. For example, Stephen P. Brown has said that the "hard vs. soft sf argument .... has been done to death for years without anything of any real significance coming out of it, in my opinion" (Letter to Gary Westfahl). However, applying my research in the critical commentaries regarding hard science fiction, coupled with what I have learned from selected texts in the subgenre, I would argue for the following as a description of hard science fiction as that category has existed and has been commonly understood to date:

A hard science fiction story is a science fiction story with these special characteristics:

1. The author characteristically identifies herself as a hard science fiction writer and consciously writes for an audience of hard science fiction readers.

2. The author claims to employ scientific information and the process of scientific thinking to develop and/or support all speculative aspects of her story.

3. The author is willing to fully explain her use of scientific information and scientific thinking in explicit language, either in the text of her story or in materials accompanying or outside of the text of her story.

4. That language can be, and will be, examined by independent scientific experts and verified by them as generally accurate and logical, given the state of knowledge at the time of the story's composition.

5. Hard science fiction stories typically take one of two forms: the careful projection of near-future possibilities, or the extravagant creation of a strange or immense environment that is nonetheless scientifically possible.

A few words of explanation: The first criterion may seem unimportant, but I believe it is a key characteristic that is woefully neglected in most efforts to define hard science fiction, and one that demands extended comment. Hard science fiction is a highly contextualized activity: Writers realize that they are writing hard science fiction, and they write expecting to read by people who appreciate hard science fiction. In particular, hard science fiction writers anticipate an audience of readers who know a great deal about science and are prepared—even willing—to point out scientific inaccuracies in stories. As David Brin notes, "[T]here is a community of hard SF readers and writers 'out there,' ready to judge a work by very exacting standards of verisimilitude" ("Running Out of Speculative Niches" 10). Indeed, the fact is that hard science fiction writers characteristically write with the expectation that their works will be so "judged"—that is the "game" of hard science fiction. And since this interplay between author and reader evolved only in the science fiction magazines, hard science fiction must be regarded as a relatively recent development.

Furthermore, since this is a relationship that can only be founded within the modern tradition of self-conscious science fiction—"genre science fiction," to some—it is one that can emerge only imperfectly in texts outside of that tradition. Certainly, Jules Verne achieved some temporary success in forging such a relationship: He anticipated the characteristic attitude of the hard science fiction writer in his efforts to be scrupulously accurate in his scientific facts, and he discovered or created an audience of readers who cared about meeting such standards and would upbraid Verne for failing to meet them. Still, he did not manage to *sustain* that relationship: Even Arthur B. Evans concedes that his readers' concerns for science were "less so in his later" novels (Letter to Gary Westfahl); indeed, Verne's later tendency to drift into historical fiction or into more fantastic projections may reflect his own lessening concern for scientific accuracy; and Verne's successors in writing fantastic fiction, and their readers, apparently did not maintain a similar level of concern about scientific accuracy.

In the sketch of the development of hard science fiction that I am offering, the form emerges not so much from writers as from readers: readers trained by Gernsback and Campbell to be attentive to matters of scientific detail and to protest loudly when scientific errors occurred in stories. The natural result would be writers who shared and responded to this concern—first Hal Clement and Arthur C. Clarke, and later many others.

In some critical circles, the preceding comments will seem quaint and old-fashioned; I am attempting to characterize a work by its author's "intent." Yet this methodology does not strike me as suspect when there is, as in this case, an abundance of testimony from relevant writers testifying to this intent and an abundance of evidence from readers acknowledging their recognition of this intent. Efforts to define hard science fiction with reference only to features in the text will necessarily grow expansive and ultimately useless. Innumerable stories in all genres can be located that display some knowledge of and respect for scientific accuracy, yet to accept all of these as hard science fiction both renders the term almost meaningless and ignores the historically narrow application of the term. To begin by describing hard science fiction as the result of a conscious effort to produce hard science fiction stories for an audience of hard science fiction readers yields a body of texts that is closely congruent to the actual body of texts universally identified as hard science fiction.[4]

Of course, if this is the *only* thing that one can say about hard science fiction—that it is a form of writing consciously practiced by writers and consciously appreciated by readers—then one has not really said enough to describe the subgenre; perhaps it is only a sort of shared illusion, a category that really has no grounds to exist. The rest of my description, then, attempts to establish that there are in fact reasons why writers and readers can logically regard hard science fiction as a separable subgenre.

The second criterion should really be no surprise, since it is found in scores of other attempts to define the subgenre. The added element here is that hard science fiction is best characterized by the claim, and not necessarily the substance, of scientific accuracy, and the insistence that the goal is to have *all* aspects of the story have this kind of scientific support.

The use of *claims to employ*, rather than the stronger *employs*, simply establishes that there are three separable defining characteristics here: that the author announces her use of science, that she describes her use of science, and that her use of science can be independently verified as accurate. The issues are separable because if an author employs impeccable scientific data and logic without announcing that she is doing so, and/or without describing her data and logic in detail, she cannot be accepted as a hard science fiction writer—just as a researcher who absolutely refuses to announce and explain her experimental methods cannot be accepted as a true scientist.

The third criterion of explicit explanatory language has, in part, been recognized by previous commentators, as seen in Isaac Asimov's description of hard science fiction as "stories in which the details of science play an important role and in which the author is accurate about those details, too, and takes the trouble to explain them clearly" (Introduction to "Neutron Star" 299). What has not been noted, I believe, until this study, is that hard science fiction writers are characteristically loquacious in describing the science in their stories outside of those stories. I would argue, in fact, that virtually all major writers accepted as hard science fiction writers have, at some time, offered some explanation of their methodology in creating some of their stories—either in the text of those stories or in accompanying articles or afterwords. And I would maintain that that consistent willingness to put their cards on the table, so to speak, can be seen as a defining characteristic of writers in the subgenre and can be seen as one clear sign that they are attempting to seem like scientists at work, even if they otherwise are not like scientists at work.

The fourth criterion attempts to define an exact process for judging what has also been long accepted as a trait of hard science fiction—that it not only appears to be scientifically accurate but is scientifically accurate. It may be true, as Gregory Benford notes, that there is at least a minor element of error in all hard science fiction stories (as cited in Huntington, "Hard-Core Science Fiction and the Illusion of Science" 50) and that hard science fiction writers may be occasionally allowed a gigantic blunder, such as Larry Niven's failure to realize that his Ringworld could not maintain a stable orbit; nevertheless, to be accepted as a hard science fiction writer, one's speculative work must be generally acceptable in the context of current scientific thought. And the process of independent evaluation I describe is not a proposal that such evaluation take place, because, as already indicated, that process is already taking place; many scientists and scientifically trained people regularly read hard science fiction, and they are more than willing to write letters pointing out errors of scientific fact and logic in the stories they read.

This explicit invitation to scientific analysis explains one tendency that has been repeatedly observed throughout this study: the desire to extend the label "hard science fiction" to writers whose works manifest few, if any, of the traditional characteristics of the subgenre. Most works of literature, including most works of science fiction, can establish their own value only by appealing to one nexus of authority, that of literary quality—whether one appreciates the story simply as "entertainment" or as a profound commentary on the human condition. Hard science fiction stories can also make that appeal, and many of its writers—Gregory Benford in particular—obviously want their works to be appreciated for their purely literary virtues. But hard science fiction stories can appeal to an entirely different nexus of authority, that of scientific quality. A hard science fiction story, uniquely, can claim to represent good science as well as good literature. Whether such claims are justifiable or not is an entirely different issue; but certainly, hard science fiction typically claims for itself this distinct sort of value, which tends to provide its stories with a special aura of authority that is both literary and scientific. Other writers, and critics who champion those other writers, thus want to be embraced as hard science fiction writers as a way to achieve that additional imprimatur of value; labeling J. G.

Ballard, Stanislaw Lem, or Ursula K. Le Guin in this way becomes a code for
asserting that these writers are more important than one might otherwise
acknowledge.[5] Or one could explain the phenomenon of expansive definition in
another, related way: by enlarging the term *hard science fiction* to include writers
who do not meet the established standards of extreme scientific accuracy, one
makes that criterion less important, so that those writers who better meet that
criterion are therefore less important. A critic craves the label *hard science
fiction* for her favorite writer, then, either so that the writer can somehow earn
the status of scientific value or as a way to de-emphasize the importance of that
status—in both cases, leveling the playing field so that writers commonly
accepted as hard science fiction writers no longer enjoy any special claims.

The fifth criterion might be said to identify tendencies in hard science fiction,
not necessarily traits; yet it is surely worth noting that the obsessive quest for
complete scientific accuracy naturally leads authors to two extremes: to describe
modest developments in the near future, where much background information can
be adapted from present-day circumstances and plans; or to start from scratch to
create an entirely new environment, where the author can be in complete control
of the situation. An intermediate challenge—say, to convincingly describe an
Earth society several centuries in the future—might involve too many variables
and uncertainties for an author to be sure about the scientific rigor of his
projections. In that sense, one can sympathize with Fred Hoyle and Geoffrey
Hoyle's complaint about the difficulty of completely envisioning a future human
civilization. Interestingly, what might be termed this middle territory—neither the
near future nor an extravagant new environment—is the characteristic focus, one
could argue, of most science fiction, since such realms offer so many exciting
possibilities for stories; yet hard science fiction authors seem driven by their own
priorities to avoid it.[6] In another way, then, the discipline of writing hard science
fiction imposes severe, yet freely chosen, limitations on its authors.

Overall, I make no great claims for this description, since it is a preliminary
effort, but I believe that it works fairly well as a description of the subgenre as
it is generally recognized: that is, almost all writers universally regarded as hard
science fiction writers will meet all of its major criteria, and almost all writers
not universally regarded as hard science fiction writers will fail to meet one of
its criteria.[7]

In describing hard science fiction, one realizes that the subgenre is in fact a
very small part of the entire field of science fiction. And as another consequence
of this work, the example of hard science fiction suggests there is a need for a
comprehensive mapping of the subgenres of science fiction as they have actually
emerged and become recognized during the modern history of the form.

The results will necessarily be messy. One will find a small number of distinct
and more or less permanent subgenres: hard science fiction, space opera, sword-
and-sorcery, and perhaps cyberpunk. There will be some temporary and unstable
categories that coalesce around certain magazines or authors—H. L. Gold's

Galaxy writers, the Lovecraft cult, and so on. Some groupings will be based more on personalities and politics than on the nature of the science fiction the writers produce. And many writers will consistently fail to fit into any of the groups.

Seeing hard science fiction as one of many small subcategories of science fiction, one is driven to another question: Why is this particular form so important, or, Why should it demand special attention? It is, properly described, not a large subgenre; as already suggested, its works do not consistently display superior literary merit; and the widespread desire to expand the term to embrace peripheral exemplars of the form, therefore, might seem both perverse and unnecessary.

Like everything else in this concluding chapter, my answers to this question are tentative; but at this time, I can see two possible reasons for regarding hard science fiction as an especially important type of science fiction. First, it has long been noted that science fiction writers use and build on the ideas of other writers; as Donald A. Wollheim said in *The Universe Makers*, "Somewhere in the early days of the literature someone invented a premise, argued it out with scientific (or more likely pseudoscientific) logic and convinced the readers. Once the argument is made, the premise is at once accepted on its own word, enters the tool shed of the science-fiction writer, and may be utilized thereafter by any craftsman without further repetition of the operational manual" (14). Certainly, then, hard science fiction may be important to the entire genre as a continuing source of new ideas; however, the role of hard science fiction is often somewhat different—to serve as a conduit of ideas from the scientific community to the science fiction community.

Robert L. Forward, for one, is perfectly frank in explaining this as his method of operation in *Dragon's Egg*:

I don't know how other science fiction writers write science fiction, but I know how *I* write it. First, I steal a world (or worlds). If I am really desperate, I will invent a world, but there are so many around for the taking that you might as well steal them. Some you may have to ask for. After all, it *was* Frank Drake that first proposed that there might be life on a neutron star .... [W]hen I asked Frank, I had no problem getting his permission to use his idea. ("When Science Writes the Fiction" 3)[8]

The way in which hard science fiction can fertilize the entire genre can be illustrated with many other examples. For instance, in 1961 a scientific paper first proposed the construction of a space elevator physically connecting the surface of the Earth to a point in geosynchronous Earth orbit; in 1979, hard science fiction writers Arthur C. Clarke and Charles Sheffield simultaneously made that idea the focus of their respective novels *The Fountains of Paradise* and *The Web between the Worlds*; and by 1989, the device was common enough so that a little-regarded writer like M. S. Murdock, writing *Rebellion 2456*, the first volume in a series of new Buck Rogers novels, could begin the story by having Buck take a ride in a space elevator without extended comment.

If this is indeed one valuable role that hard science fiction can play for the science fiction community, there are two possible developments that could threaten that role—both noted by David Brin in his essay "Running Out of Speculative Niches": first, that there will be increasingly fewer writers who are able or willing to grapple with the scientific literature—"[T]he depth of research called for in a truly innovative modern hard SF tale may seem daunting to many writers" (10); second, that the scientific community may find itself unable to suggest interesting new ideas—"[W]ill there always be exciting new frontiers of knowledge? Is it possible that we are closing in on the borders of the knowable? ... If science itself is due to plow its last fallow fields, can hard SF be far behind?" (11,12)—leading writers to abandon hard science fiction for lack of new subject matter.[9] As if responding to John J. Pierce's argument for hard science fiction—that it can generate new types of objects for aesthetic appreciation—Brin argues that very ability of the subgenre to envision new realities may become more and more limited, thus reducing the value and importance of its works.

Brin's first fear cannot be dismissed, for it is undoubtedly true that science is becoming more and more complex, and more and more inaccessible to those without formal scientific training; thus, it may be necessary to develop a new system for funneling new ideas into science fiction. One possible answer is suggested by an article by John G. Cramer in the June, 1989 issue of *Analog Science Fiction/Science Fact*, "Wormholes and Time Machines," which explains in clear terms recent theoretical work suggesting that Einstein's theory of general relativity permits the construction of a time machine, and which openly invites science fiction writers to make use of this development in their stories. In the future, then, instead of the previous route followed by the space elevator and other ideas—scientific journal to hard science fiction to other science fiction—there may be a new, more convoluted route—scientific journal to popular scientific article to hard science fiction to other science fiction.[10]

Brin's other fear may be exaggerated, for scientific developments since the time he issued his warning seem to open many new possibilities for hard science fiction in fields like information theory, genetic engineering, bionics and bioengineering, and chaos theory. One particularly exciting new idea is the prospect of creating new, pocket universes with different physical laws than our own—a development that serves as the unexpected denouément to one recent science fiction story, Walter Jon Williams's "Elegy for Angels and Dogs." This single concept in itself appears to offer virtually limitless possibilities for hard science fiction in the future.

If one can assume that hard science fiction will continue to function in its present manner, there is definitely one reason to regard it as especially important; still, while this issue is clearly of general interest to the science fiction community, this answer will not be persuasive to literary critics, who will not see in its new ideas alone any reason to pay special attention to hard science fiction—for, to state the obvious, new ideas in themselves do not make for superior fiction. Yet the priorities that motivate hard science fiction, if not all of its texts, do have special claims for critical examination.

Hard science fiction is best characterized as an intensification—perhaps a "fetishization"—of concerns and approaches that elsewhere influence the genre to a lesser extent. A traditional defense of science fiction, most forcefully stated in the comments from John W. Campbell, Jr., cited earlier, is that its concerns and approaches lead to narratives that are truly unique; a traditional argument against that defense is that those concerns and approaches in fact yield a body of literature that is not particularly unique,[11] as suggested by these remarks from Ursula K. Le Guin: "All fiction is metaphor. Science fiction is metaphor. What sets it apart from older forms of fiction seems to be its use of new metaphors, drawn from certain great dominants of our contemporary life—science, all the sciences, and technology, and the relativistic and historical outlook, among them. Space travel is one of these metaphors; so is an alternative society, an alternative biology; the future is another. The future, in fiction, is a metaphor" (Introduction [xvi]). If one accepts Campbell's viewpoint, it would seem that because of their intense concern for the peculiar dictates of science fiction, hard science fiction texts should be more likely to exhibit genuine and unsettling novelty; the fact that they usually do not, as suggested by my studies of *A Fall of Moondust*, *Mission of Gravity*, and *Between the Strokes of Night*, would appear to offer support for Le Guin's opinion.

To be sure, this fundamental question can be approached from different directions. David N. Samuelson, for example, sees one crucial issue of hard science fiction in its overarching claims of scientific veracity, which as I have already suggested conflict with the traditional authority of the reader: "The scientist's regard for scientific information as privileged, a status claimed for it in discursive non-fiction, breaks the plane of fictional reality. Asserting for science the status of truth in the world outside the frame abrogates the usual contract between creators and audiences of fiction" ("Botching the Science in Science Fiction" 100). In a sense, my description resolves the dilemma by establishing two separate criteria for evaluation: implicitly, by writing and publishing a work of fiction, a hard science fiction writer invites and demands evalation by aesthetic criteria—is it a good story? Explicitly, by claiming to be scientifically accurate and by describing her process of creation, a hard science fiction writer invites and demand evaluation by scientific criteria—does the story represent good science? So there are two judgments to make about a hard science fiction story, and split decisions are possible: One can say good story, lousy science, or lousy story, good science.

However, simply because an author invites and demands a certain type of evaluation does not mean that the author is entitled to receive that type of evaluation; and to me that is the issue that Samuelson is driving at. For example, Charles Dickens scholars, to my knowledge, do not devote a great deal of attention to the issue of whether or not his depictions of life in nineteenth-century London are historically accurate; it does not seem to be a particularly important matter. Similarly, one could argue, the issue of whether or not a given story is accurate in its scientific data and logic is also not a particularly important matter, even if the writers and readers of hard science fiction insist that it is.

The overall importance of the scientific evaluation of hard science fiction, in my view, depends on the problem I have posed. That is, if following the dictates of science indeed generates unusual or novel narratives, then consideration of the science underlying and visible in the narrative must enter into the evaluative process, as a necessary way of understanding and judging what has been created in the narrative; on the other hand, if as I have suggested the science in hard science fiction turns out to be not particularly important to the act of narrative creation, then there is no need for the evaluative process to include a separate stage of scientific analysis.

I am addressing large issues here. But based on the evidence I have accumulated, I am presently inclined to offer a skeptical response to claims for the unique value of hard science fiction.

From the standpoint of literature, the scientific demands of hard science fiction—complete fidelity to known scientific facts and unfailing rigor in developing scientific ideas—constitute an artificial constraint on the process of narrative creation, comparable to writing a novel in which characters' inner thoughts are never expressed or in which characters never speak in complete sentences. At times, such constraints might inspire writers to unexpected brilliance; at times, they might force writers into grievous aesthetic flaws; and at times, they may have no appreciable effect on the story. In the case of hard science fiction, of course, the constraints can supply a special form of extraliterary pleasure to writers and certain readers—the challenge of avoiding scientific errors, and the challenge of discovering scientific errors—but these are not pleasures available to the majority of hard science fiction readers. Overall, it seems hard to claim that such constraints are either valuable or damaging to the process of writing fiction.

One might also defend hard science fiction as a uniquely valuable form of scientific thought, in the manner of Campbell; however, from the standpoint of science, the literary demands of hard science fiction—crafting a well-written and involving narrative to accompany their imaginative ideas—constitute an artificial constraint on the process of scientific creation. We know that Albert Einstein developed his theory of relativity in part by means of thought-experiments featuring trains that ran at relativistic speeds. Would his thinking have been improved if he had felt the additional need to create an interesting story involving characters on board those trains? At times, this added mental exercise might have helped to clarify or strengthen his insights; at times, it might have interfered with his process of scientific deduction; and at times, it might have had no effect on his work. Overall, it seems hard to claim that such efforts would either improve or harm the processes of scientific thought. Thus, it seems, there is no unique value in hard science fiction either from the standpoint of literature or from the standpoint of science.

Of course, this may not be the final answer. The apparent absence of true novelty in hard science fiction may be attributed in part, as I have indicated, to flaws in the process of writing hard science fiction considered as a genuinely scientific experiment. If those flaws are addressed and corrected, the possible uniqueness of hard science fiction becomes a testable hypothesis. That is, strictly following the procedure already suggested, critics might recruit scientists to generate possible new ideas for science fiction stories; they could recruit writers to produce stories based on those ideas without regard to aesthetic merit or market viability and could examine the resulting stories to see if the same scientific ideas do in fact tend to lead different writers in the same unexpected directions. Then and only then, perhaps, will we see the true possibilities in hard science fiction.

I am now prepared, finally, to offer my own answers to the questions that were posed in the first paragraph of this book. Hard science fiction can, and should be, clearly defined as a form of science fiction characterized by unusual attentiveness to scientific fact and thinking during all stages of the writing process and by the expectation that the results will be evaluated by readers who share those priorities. As such, it is a relatively small, and relatively recent, subgenre of science fiction. However, except for its defining traits, hard science fiction does not seem significantly different from its less scientific relatives; rather, it shares all the possibilities, and faces all the limitations, of other forms of science fiction. These are not necessarily judgments that I am pleased to offer. However, to the best of my ability, and with as much objectivity as I can muster, I have examined a wide range of evidence and have followed those pieces of evidence to their logical conclusion, regardless of my personal preferences. In short, and as is only appropriate, I have attempted to follow the philosophy that purportedly governs the writing of hard science fiction.

NOTES

1. See, for example, George Slusser's "The Ideal Worlds of Science Fiction" for an interesting and insightful explication of this posited conflict.

2. In addition to the cited remarks from "On Science Fiction," there is first of all Lewis's unfinished response to a critical review by J. B. S. Haldane (only published after his death in *Of Other Worlds*), where he said: "My science is usually wrong. Why, yes .... I needed for my purposes just enough popular astronomy to create in

'the common reader' a 'willing suspension of disbelief'. No one hopes, in such fantasies, to satisfy a real scientist .... There is thus a great deal of scientific falsehood in my stories: some of it known to be false even by me when I wrote the books" ("A Reply to Professor Haldane" 75-76). Needless to say, this is antithetical to the credo of the hard science fiction writer. One could also note his comment to Brian W. Aldiss and Kingsley Amis: "I'm no scientist and not interested in the purely technical side of it" ("Unreal Estates" 87).

3. I use the term *description* instead of *definition* because the latter word carries the connotation of limits that are definite and timeless; and since literary genres continually evolve and change, a *definition* of a genre is in a sense impossible. Still, it might be possible to offer a *description* of the genre as it has existed to date, leaving open the possibility of future changes and new developments.

4. Since *intent* is such a despised term in some critical circles, I will elaborate on this point. First, it can hardly be denied that before and during their writing, *writers have intentions*, because they verbosely announce those intentions—sometimes before the work is completed, demonstrating (if it needs demonstrating) that their intentions are genuine and not merely after-the-fact inventions to mask an essentially random creative process. Even taciturn authors may demonstrate their intentions in certain ways, notably the places they submit their manuscripts: A writer who sends a story to *Isaac Asimov's Science Fiction Magazine* makes a statement about her intentions, just like a writer who submits a story to *The New Yorker*.

Second, if we have access to explicit and implicit statements about authors' intentions, *it becomes possible to classify literary works according to those intentions*. That is, one can create a group of texts called A characterized by the fact that their authors all intended to write a type of work called A, and a group of texts called B characterized by the fact that their authors all intended to write a type of work called B. And that is one way to explain the general way I prefer to describe literary genres, particularly science fiction in general and, here, hard science fiction.

These first two points strike me as inarguably true; but my own approach depends on a third, less certain principle: *Grouping texts by authors' intentions creates meaningful literary categories*. One can easily maintain that, yes, a critic *could* classify works by authors' intentions, but that the process would produce only arbitrary and useless categories, making it a system akin to the equally possible tasks of classifying works by the predominant color on their covers or by the number of chapters they contain. This third point, then, must be considered a hypothesis, one that might be proved or disproved in particular cases by examining the works in the derived categories and determining whether there are in fact meaningful relationships between those works and shared characteristics that are not found in texts outside those categories. And based on my own reading in the field, I strongly suspect that this is true in the cases of science fiction and hard science fiction.

5. There is, one could argue, a wonderful historical irony here. In the 1930s and 1940s, editors like Gernsback and Campbell labored to imbue science fiction with the aura of scientific respectability, and their efforts were not without results; in the 1950s, many people had accepted the notion that science fiction could be in some ways educational regarding science, and I am sure, for example, that my parents' willingness to support my young interest in science fiction stemmed in part from a

belief that my reading it was beneficial in this way. But commentators in the 1950s and 1960s—Damon Knight, James Blish, Judith Merril, Michael Moorcock, Harlan Ellison—either minimized or belittled the issue of scientific accuracy in science fiction; surely, in crafting "speculative fiction" of genuine literary merit, that was hardly an important issue. However, what they failed to realize is that while removing science as an issue in science fiction did open the door to, say, J. G. Ballard, it also opened the door to *Star Trek, Star Wars, Space Invaders,* and other, less admirable efforts that altogether served to destroy any reputation science fiction might have had for its scientific value. Today, I am sure, no parents believe that their children will derive any educational benefits from science fiction. Now, as if missing the aura of science that Gernsback and Campbell once provided, critics employ the term *hard science fiction* as a way to provide certain works with that aura and seem to resent it when some favorite authors are denied that description. Of course, if the term *science fiction* still carried any scientific weight, it would not be necessary to dignify authors with the additional label of *hard science fiction.*

6. This is not to say that hard science fiction never deals with such scenarios—one could maintain, for example, that Clarke's *Imperial Earth* and some of Gregory Benford's novels occupy this ground—but the relative paucity of these intermediate stories suggests that there are indeed reasons why hard science fiction is characteristically either microcosmic or macrocosmic. Also, to an extent, these two forms may also arise from an author's desire to employ familiar general models: Attempting to adapt forms like the detective story, disaster novel, or spy thriller, a writer might be naturally inclined to choose a near-future and familiar environment; while attempting to adapt forms like the travel tale and heroic fantasy, a writer might be naturally inclined to create a deliberately exotic environment. A projected story between these two extremes could pose more difficulties, particularly to authors who often claim to have little interest in literary issues per se, and who thus might be interested in types of stories that involve no problematic choices in genre.

7. One could compare this definition to the one offered by Hal Clement, discussed in the third chapter, which implicitly echoes some of my own points, including the fact that it is a "recognizable" field and that an author must explain herself—"have an impressive-sounding excuse" ("Hard Sciences and Tough Technologies" 51).

8. And Forward himself, before and during his career as a science fiction writer, helped many science fiction writers as a scientist; Larry Niven, for example, has related how Forward helped him create the Smoke Ring for *The Integral Trees* (in "Blowing Smoke").

9. Brin makes this point more explicitly in "On Niven": "If you think that the territory of notions is limited, then the hard sf writer is like a wildcat miner drilling out resources that are shrinking. For whatever it's worth, some people think that way. A lot of sf writers aren't writing hard science fiction because they think most of it has been written" (3).

10. The fact that Cramer is also a hard science fiction writer creates another possibility: that persons who in the past might have turned to hard science fiction may in the future fulfill their speculative urges simply by writing articles about their ideas. This is one possible way to characterize the later career of Campbell, who

stopped writing stories and started writing editorial essays. In *Collected Editorials from Analog*, for example, editor Harry Harrison argues that Campbell's editorial "Space for Industry" is virtually a kind of science fiction story that happens to take a non-narrative form.

11. In "The Dance with Darkness," I examine the potential novelty of science fiction from the viewpoint of sociobiology, suggesting that there may indeed be biological imperatives that drive literature toward conventional patterns, but leaving open the chance, based on a few unconventional science fiction stories, that the process of writing science fiction can indeed help writers break away from those patterns.

Bibliography

This bibliography only lists works cited in the text; additional works with some relevance to the subject of hard science fiction are listed in David N. Samuelson's "On Hard Science Fiction: A Bibliography," *Science-Fiction Studies*, 20 (July 1993): 149-156. When more than one essay in a volume are cited, individual entries identify the source only by book title and last name of author or editor(s); complete bibliographical data is provided in a separate entry under the name of the author or editor(s).

Aldiss, Brian W. *The Shape of Further Things: Speculation on Change*. 1970. London: Corgi Books, 1974.

————, with David Wingrove. *Trillion Year Spree: The History of Science Fiction*. New York: Atheneum, 1986. A previous version, as by Aldiss alone, was *Billion Year Spree: The True History of Science Fiction*. New York: Schocken Books, 1973.

Aldiss, Brian W., editor. *All about Venus*. New York: Dell Books, 1968. Published in England as *Farewell, Fantastic Venus!*

Allen, L. David. *Science Fiction: An Introduction*. *Cliffs Notes*. Lincoln, Nebraska: Cliffs Notes, Incorporated, 1973.

Anderson, Poul. "The Creation of Imaginary Worlds: The World Builder's Handbook and Pocket Companion." In *Science Fiction: Today and Tomorrow*, edited by Bretnor, 235-257.

————. "Geology, Meteorology, Oceanography, Geography, Nomenclature, Biology." In *Medea: Harlan's World*, edited by Ellison, 17-27.

————. Interview with Jeffrey M. Elliot. In *Science Fiction Voices #2*, 41-50. Interview originally published in *Galileo* in 1979.

————. Letter. In "Brass Tacks." *Analog Science Fact/Science Fiction*, 67 (May 1961): 172-174.

————. "Nature: Laws and Surprises." In *Mindscapes: The Geographies of*

Imagined Worlds. Edited by George E. Slusser and Eric S. Rabkin. Carbondale, Illinois: Southern Illinois University Press, 1989, 3-15.

——————. "The Science." In *Nebula Award Stories Seven*. Edited by Lloyd Biggle, Jr. New York: Harper & Row, Publishers, 1973, 263-273.

——————. "Star-flights and Fantasies: Sagas Still to Come." In *The Craft of Science Fiction*, edited by Bretnor, 22-35.

——————. *Tau Zero*. Garden City: Doubleday and Company, 1970.

Anthony, Piers, and Robert E. Margroff. *The Ring*. New York: Ace Books, 1968.

Asimov, Isaac. "Afterword" to "The Talking Stone." In *Asimov's Mysteries*. By Isaac Asimov. 1968. New York: Dell Books, 1969, 53-54.

——————. Introduction to "Neutron Star." In *Stories from the Hugo Winners, Volume II*. Edited by Isaac Asimov. 1971. New York: Fawcett Crest Books, 1973, 299-300.

——————. "Science Fiction Today." In *The Tyrannosaurus Prescription*. By Isaac Asimov. Buffalo, New York: Prometheus Press, 1989, 289-293. Essay originally published in 1988.

——————. "There's Nothing Like a Good Foundation." In *Asimov on Science Fiction*. By Isaac Asimov. 1981. New York: Avon Books, 1982, 281-285.

Bainbridge, William Sims. *Dimensions of Science Fiction*. Cambridge, Massachusetts: Harvard University Press, 1986.

Barron, Neil. *Anatomy of Wonder: Science Fiction*. New York: R. R. Bowker, 1976.

Benford, Gregory. "Effing the Ineffable." In *Aliens: The Anthropology of Science Fiction*. Edited by George Slusser and Eric S. Rabkin. Carbondale and Edwardsville, Illinois: Southern Illinois University Press, 1987, 13-25.

——————. Interview with Jeffrey M. Elliot. In *Science Fiction Voices #3*, 44-52.

——————. "Is There a Technological Fix for the Human Condition?" In *Hard Science Fiction*, edited by Slusser and Rabkin, 82-98.

——————. "Real Science, Imaginary Worlds." In *The Ascent of Wonder*, edited by Hartwell and Cramer, 15-23.

——————. "Science and Science Fiction." In *Science Fiction: The Academic Awakening*, edited by McNelly, 30-34.

——————. "Time and *Timescape*." *Science-Fiction Studies* 20 (July 1993): 184-190.

Blish, James. "Books." *The Magazine of Fantasy and Science Fiction* 39 (August 1970): 58-62.

——————. [writing as William Atheling, Jr.] "The Fens Revisited: 'Said' Books and Incest." In *The Issue at Hand*. By James Blish. Chicago: Advent Publishers, 1964, 109-114. Originally published in *Axe* (August 1962).

——————. [writing as William Atheling, Jr.] "Science-Fantasy and Translations: Two More Cans of Worms." In *More Issues at Hand*. By James Blish. Chicago: Advent Publishers, 1970, 98-116. First published in 1960 and 1963.

Bova, Ben. "Inside *Analog* or How I Learned to Stop Worrying and Love My Job." In *Viewpoint*. By Ben Bova. A Boskone Book. Cambridge, Massachusetts: New England Science Fiction Association, 1977, 1-10.

——————. "Introduction: Letter to the Author." In *Unaccompanied Sonata*. By Orson Scott Card. New York: Dell Books, 1981, 15-19.

Bretnor, Reginald. "The Future of Science Fiction." In *Modern Science Fiction*, edited by Bretnor, 265-294.

————. "Science Fiction in the Age of Space." In *Science Fiction: Today and Tomorrow*, edited by Bretnor, 150-178.

————, ed. *The Craft of Science Fiction*. New York: Harper & Row, Publishers, 1976.

————. *Modern Science Fiction: Its Meaning and Its Future*. New York: Coward-McCann, 1953.

————. *Science Fiction: Today and Tomorrow*. Baltimore, Maryland: Penguin Books, 1974.

Brin, David. "Running Out of Speculative Niches: A Crisis for Hard Science Fiction?" In *Hard Science Fiction*, edited by Slusser and Rabkin, 8-13.

Brin, David; Gregory Benford; Wendy All; John Hertz; Steven Barnes; and Frederik Pohl. "On Niven." In *N-Space*, by Niven, 3-13.

Brosnan, John. "*A for Andromeda*." In *The Science Fiction Encyclopedia*, edited by Nicholls, 17-19.

Brown, Stephen. Letter to Gary Westfahl. August 15, 1992.

Budrys, Algis. *Benchmarks: Galaxy Bookshelf*. Carbondale and Edwardsville, Illinois: Southern Illinois University Press, 1985.

————. "Books." *The Magazine of Fantasy and Science Fiction* 56 (May 1979): 19-8.

————. "March, 1969." In *Benchmarks*, by Budrys, 200-205. Originally published in *Galaxy* (March 1969).

————. "March, 1971." In *Benchmarks*, by Budrys, 296-301. Originally published in *Galaxy* (March 1971).

————. "October, 1967." In *Benchmarks*, by Budrys, 121-127. Originally published in *Galaxy* (October 1967).

Campbell, John W., Jr. "Introduction." In *The Man Who Sold the Moon*. By Robert A. Heinlein. Chicago: Shasta Publishers, 1950, 11-15.

————. "Introduction." In *Who Goes There?* By John W. Campbell, Jr. Chicago: Shasta Publishing Company, 1948, 3-6.

————. *The John W. Campbell Letters, Volume I*. Edited by Perry A. Chapdelaine, Sr., Tony Chapdelaine, and George Hay. Franklin, Tennessee: AC Projects, 1985.

————. Letter to Hal Clement [Harry Clement Stubbs]. April 12, 1953. In *The John W. Campbell Letters, Volume I*, edited by Chapdelaine, Chapdelaine, and Hay, 149-151.

————. Letter to Jack Williamson. January 7, 1971. In *The John W. Campbell Letters, Volume I*, edited by Chapdelaine, Chapdelaine, and Hay, 592-593.

————. Letter to Ronald E. Graham. September 8, 1969. In *John W. Campbell: An Australian Tribute*. Edited by John Bangsund. Canberra, Australia: Ronald E. Graham and John Bangsund, 1974 [text incorrectly gives publication year as 1972].

————. "The Old Navy Game." *Astounding Science-Fiction* 25 (June 1940): 6.

————. "The Perfect Machine." *Astounding Science-Fiction* 25 (May 1940): 5.

————. "Science Fiction and the Opinion of the Universe." *Saturday Review* 39 (May 12, 1956): 9-10, 42-43.

————. "We Can't Keep Up!" *Astounding Science-Fiction* 26 (October 1940): 6.

Carr, Terry. "The Dance of the Changer and the Three." 1968. In *World's Best*

Science Fiction 1969. Edited by Donald A. Wollheim and Terry Carr. New York: Ace Books, 1969, 259-274.

Carter, Paul. "You Can Write Science Fiction if You Want To." In *Hard Science Fiction*, edited by Slusser and Rabkin, 141-151.

Clarke, Arthur C. *A Fall of Moondust*. New York: Harcourt Brace Jovanovich, 1961.

——————. "Foreword" to the 1961 edition of *Prelude to Space*. 1961. In *Prelude to Space*. [this edition published as *The Space Dreamers*]. New York: Lancer Books, 1969, 5-7. Novel originally published in 1951.

——————. *The Ghost from the Grand Banks*. New York: Bantam Books, 1990.

——————. *Prelude to Space*. New York: Galaxy Novels, 1951.

——————. *2061: Odyssey Three*. New York: Del Rey/Ballantine Books, 1987.

Clement, Hal. "Author's Afterword." In *The Best of Hal Clement*, by Clement, 372-79.

——————. *The Best of Hal Clement*. Edited by Lester del Rey. New York: Del Rey/Ballantine Books, 1979.

——————. "The Creation of Imaginary Beings."   In *Science Fiction: Today and Tomorrow*, edited by Bretnor, 259-275.

——————. "Hard Sciences and Tough Technologies." In *The Craft of Science Fiction*, edited by Bretnor, 37-52.

——————. Interview with Darrell Schweitzer. In *Science Fiction Voices #1*. By Darrell Schweitzer. San Bernardino, California: Borgo Press, 1979. Interview originally published in *Amazing Science Fiction* in 1977.

——————. Letter. In "Brass Tacks." *Analog: Science Fact/Science Fiction* 67 (May 1961): 171-172.

——————. *Mission of Gravity*. 1953. Garden City: Doubleday and Company, 1954. Originally published in *Astounding Science-Fiction* in 1953.

——————. "Whirligig World." *Astounding Science-Fiction* 51 (June 1953): 102-114.

Clute, John. "Hal Clement." In *The Science Fiction Encyclopedia*, edited by Nicholls, 123-124.

Clute, John, and Peter Nicholls. "Fred Hoyle." In *The Science Fiction Encyclopedia*, edited by Nicholls, 295.

——————, eds. *The Encyclopedia of Science Fiction*. New York: St. Martin's Press, 1993.

Collings, Michael. "Science and Scientism in C. S. Lewis's *That Hideous Strength*." In *Hard Science Fiction*, edited by Slusser and Rabkin, 131-140.

Cramer, John G. "The Alternate View: Wormholes and Time Machines." *Analog Science Fiction/Science Fact* 109 (June 1989): 124-128.

Davenport, Basil. *Inquiry into Science Fiction*. New York: Longman, Green, and Co., 1955.

del Rey, Lester.   "Introduction: Hal Clement, Rationalist."   In *The Best of Hal Clement*, by Clement, pxi-xvii.

Disch, Thomas M. "The Embarrassments of Science Fiction." In *Science Fiction at Large*, edited by Nicholls, 141-155.

"Discussions" [Readers' letters and responses]. *Amazing Stories* 1 (January 1927): 974.

"Discussions." *Amazing Stories* 1 (February 1927): 1077.

Edwards, Malcolm J. "P. Schuyler Miller." In *The Encyclopedia of Science Fiction*, edited by Clute and Nicholls, 808-809.

Elliot, Jeffrey M. *Science Fiction Voices #2*. San Bernardino, California: Borgo Press, 1979.

—————. *Science Fiction Voices #3*. San Bernardino, California: Borgo Press, 1980.

Ellison, Harlan. *The Book of Ellison*. Edited by Andrew Porter. New York: ALGOL Press, 1978.

—————. "Cosmic Hod-Carriers." In *Medea: Harlan's World*, edited by Ellison, 1-7.

—————. "A Few (Hopefully Final) Words on 'The New Wave.'" In *Science Fiction: The Academic Awakening*, edited by McNelly, 40-43.

—————. "Introduction to 'The Jigsaw Man.'" In *Dangerous Visions #2*. Edited by Harlan Ellison. 1966. New York: Berkley Books, 1969, 70-71.

—————. "A Time for Daring." In *The Book of Ellison*, by Harlan Ellison, 101-115. Essay originally published in *ALGOL* (March 1967).

—————. "20 March 70." In *The Other Glass Teat: Further Essays of Opinion on Television*. By Harlan Ellison. New York: Pyramid Books, 1975, 38-43.

—————. "A Voice from the Styx." In *The Book of Ellison*, by Harlan Ellison, 117-40. Essay originally published in *Psychotic* (January and September 1968).

—————, ed. *Medea: Harlan's World*. New York: Bantam Books, 1985.

Elrick, George S. *Science Fiction Handbook for Readers and Writers*. Chicago: Chicago Review Press, 1978.

Evans, Arthur B. Letter to Gary Westfahl, January 28, 1995.

Flynn, Michael F. "The Washer at the Ford." *Analog Science Fiction/Science Fact* 109 (June 1989): 14-70; (July 1989): 126-176.

Forward, Robert F. "When Science Writes the Fiction." In *Hard Science Fiction*, edited by Slusser and Rabkin, 1-7.

Gernsback, Hugo. "Amazing Creations." *Amazing Stories* 2 (May 1927): 109.

—————. "$500.00 Prize Story Contest." *Amazing Stories* 1 (December 1926): 773.

—————. Introduction to "Ten Million Miles Sunward" [unsigned]. *Amazing Stories* 2 (March 1928): 1127

—————. "Introduction to This Story" [unsigned]. [*Off on a Comet*]. *Amazing Stories* 1 (April 1926): 4-5.

—————. "The Magnetic Storm." 1917. *Amazing Stories* 1 (June 1926): 350-356. Originally published in *Science and Invention* in 1917.

—————. "A New Sort of Magazine." *Amazing Stories* 1 (April 1926): 3.

—————. "Plausibility in Scientifiction." *Amazing Stories* 1 (November 1926): 675.

—————. "Science Fiction vs. Science Faction." *Wonder Stories Quarterly* 2 (fall 1930): 5.

Godwin, Tom. "The Cold Equations." In *The Science Fiction Hall of Fame*. Edited by Robert Silverberg. 1970. New York: Avon Books, 1971, 543-569. Story originally published in *Astounding Science-Fiction* in 1954.

Grant, C. L. "Introduction: Getting Your Feet Wet." In *Writing and Selling Science Fiction*, by the Science Fiction Writers of America, 1-31.

Guffey, George. "Noise, Information, and Statistics in Stanislaw Lem's *The Investigation*." In *Hard Science Fiction*, edited by Slusser and Rabkin, 164-176.

Gunn, James. "The Readers of Hard Science Fiction." In *Hard Science Fiction*, edited by Slusser and Rabkin, 70-81.

Hartwell, David G., and Kathryn Cramer, eds. *The Ascent of Wonder: The Evolution of Hard Science Fiction*. New York: TOR Books, 1994.

Hassler, Donald M. "Ambivalence Towards 'Classes' or 'Genres': A Yoking of Anthony Trollope and Hal Clement." Paper presented at the 16th Annual Eaton Conference on Science Fiction and Fantasy Literature, Riverside, California, April, 1994.

————. *Comic Tones in Science Fiction: The Art of Compromise with Nature*. Westport, Connecticut: Greenwood Press, 1982.

————. *Hal Clement. Starmont Reader's Guide 11*. Mercer Island, Washington: Starmont House, 1982.

Heinlein, Robert A. "Goldfish Bowl." 1942. In *The Menace from Earth*, by Robert A. Heinlein. 1959. New York: Signet Books, 1962, 129-158. Story originally published in *Astounding Science-Fiction* in 1942.

————. "On the Writing of Speculative Fiction." In *Of Worlds Beyond: The Science of Science Fiction Writing*. Edited by Lloyd Arthur Eshbach, 1947. Chicago: Advent Publishers, 1964, 13-19.

————. "Science Fiction: Its Nature, Faults, and Virtues." In *The Science Fiction Novel: Imagination and Social Criticism*. Edited by Basil Davenport. 1959. Chicago: Advent Publishers, 1969, 14-48. Based on a lecture delivered at the University of Chicago, February 8, 1957.

————. "Solution Unsatisfactory." 1940. In *Expanded Universe: The New Worlds of Robert A. Heinlein*. New York: Ace Books, 1980, 96-144. Story originally published in *Astounding Science-Fiction* in 1940.

Hollow, John. *Against the Night, the Stars: The Science Fiction of Arthur C. Clarke*. 1976. New York: Harcourt Brace Jovanovich, 1983.

Hoyle, Fred, and Geoffrey Hoyle. "Preface" to *Fifth Planet*. 1963. New York: Crest Books, 1964, 1963, v-vii.

Huntington, John. "Hard-Core Science Fiction and the Illusion of Science." In *Hard Science Fiction*, edited by Slusser and Rabkin, 45-57.

Knight, Damon. *In Search of Wonder*. Second Edition, Revised and Enlarged. Chicago: Advent: Publishers, 1967. First edition published in 1956.

————. "Stranger Station." 1956. In *SF: The Best of the Best*. Edited by Judith Merril. 1967. New York: Dell Books, 1968, 143-168.

Korshak, Melvin. "Introduction: Trends in Modern Science-Fiction." In *The Best Science Fiction Stories: 1949*. Edited by Everett C. Bleiler and T. E. Dikty. New York: Frederick Fell, Inc., 1949, 11-18.

Le Guin, Ursula K. "Introduction." In *The Left Hand of Darkness*. New York: Ace Books, 1976, [xi-xvi]. Novel originally published in 1969.

Lewis, Anthony. "Magazine Reviews." *Locus*, no. 30 (January 1969): [5-7].

Lewis, C. S. *Of Other Worlds: Essays and Stories*. Edited, with a Preface, by Walter Hooper. New York: Harcourt Brace Jovanovich, 1966.

————. "On Science Fiction." In *Of Other Worlds*, by Lewis, 59-73. Originally presented as a talk to the Cambridge University English Club on November 24, 1955.

————. "A Reply to Professor Haldane." In *Of Other Worlds*, by Lewis, 74-85.

Lewis, C. S., Kingsley Amis, and Brian W. Aldiss. "Unreal Estates" [a recorded conversation]. In *Of Other Worlds*, by Lewis, 86-96. First published in *SF Horizons*, no. 1 (spring 1964): as "The Establishment Must Die and Rot ... "

Malzberg, Barry N. "SF Forever." In *The Engines of the Night: Science Fiction in the Eighties*. 1982. New York: Bluejay Books, 1984, 165-166. Essay originally written in 1980.

Martin, George R. R. "First, Sew on a Tentacle (Recipes for Believable Aliens)." In *Writing and Selling Science Fiction*, by the Science Fiction Writers of America, 147-166.

McCaffrey, Anne. "Hitch Your Dragon to a Star: Romance and Glamour in Science Fiction." In *Science Fiction: Today and Tomorrow*, edited by Bretnor, 278-292.

McConnell, Frank. "Sturgeon's Law: First Corollary." In *Hard Science Fiction*, edited by Slusser and Rabkin, 14-23.

McGuff, Luke ["with assist from Jane Hawkins and Vonda N. McIntyre"]. Letter. *Science Fiction Eye*, no. 9 (November 1991): 10-11.

McGuirk, Carol. "The 'New' Romancers: Science Fiction Innovators from Gernsback to Gibson." In *Fiction Two Thousand: Cyberpunk and the Future of Narrative*. Edited by George Slusser and Tom Shippey. Athens: University of Georgia Press, 1992, 109-129.

McNelly, Willis E, editor. *Science Fiction: The Academic Awakening*. Associate Editors Jane Hipolito and A. James Stupple. A CEA Chap Book. Shreveport, Louisiana: College English Association, 1974.

Merril, Judith. "Books." *The Magazine of Fantasy and Science Fiction* 29 (October 1965): 92-98.

————. "Books." *The Magazine of Fantasy and Science Fiction* 31 (August 1966): 57-69.

————. "Books." *The Magazine of Fantasy and Science Fiction* 32 (January 1967): 63-70.

Merril, Judith, with Fritz Leiber. "Books." *The Magazine of Fantasy and Science Fiction* 30 (June 1966): 32-40.

————, ed. *SF 12*. New York: Delacorte Press, 1968.

Miller, P. Schuyler. "Book Review." *Astounding Science-Fiction* 40 (October 1947): 104-06.

————. "Book Reviews." *Astounding Science-Fiction* 44 (September 1949): 150-53.

————. "Book Reviews." *Astounding Science-Fiction* 46 (November 1950): 93-94.

————. "The Reference Library." *Astounding Science-Fiction* 52 (December 1953): 140-151.

————. "The Reference Library." *Astounding Science-Fiction* 52 (January 1954): 143-150.

————. "The Reference Library." *Astounding Science-Fiction* 53 (May 1954): 145-50.

————. "The Reference Library." *Astounding Science-Fiction* 53 (July 1954): 143-51.

————. "The Reference Library." *Astounding Science-Fiction* 54 (October 1954): 142-149.

————. "The Reference Library."*Astounding Science-Fiction* 54 (November 1954): 141-155.

————. "The Reference Library." *Astounding Science Fiction* 57 (July 1956): 148-60.

————. "The Reference Library."*Astounding Science Fiction* 57 (November 1956): 152-158.

————. "The Reference Library." *Astounding Science Fiction* 59 (May 1957): 146-50.

————. "The Reference Library." *Astounding Science Fiction* 59 (July 1957): 142-53.

————. "The Reference Library." *Astounding Science Fiction* 60 (September 1957): 141-150.

————. "The Reference Library."*Astounding Science Fiction* 60 (November 1957): 142-149.

————. "The Reference Library." *Astounding Science Fiction* 62 (February 1959): 137-149.

————. "The Reference Library." *Astounding Science Fiction* 63 (July 1959): 147-58.

————. "The Reference Library." *Astounding Science Fiction* 63 (August 1959): 146-155.

————. "The Reference Library." *Astounding Science Fiction* 64 (October 1959): 139-148.

————. "The Reference Library." *Astounding Science Fiction* 64 (January 1960): 168-176.

————. "The Reference Library." *Astounding Science Fiction* 64 (February 1960): 160-170.

————. "The Reference Library." *Analog Science Fact/Science Fiction* 67 (July 1961): 151-161.

————. "The Reference Library." *Analog Science Fact/Science Fiction* 67 (September 1961): 161-171.

————. "The Reference Library."*Analog Science Fact/Science Fiction* 68 (October 1961): 161-170.

————. "The Reference Library." *Analog Science Fact/Science Fiction* 68 (November 1961): 160-170.

————. "The Reference Library."*Analog Science Fact/Science Fiction* 68 (January 1962): 156-164.

————. "The Reference Library." *Analog Science Fact/Science Fiction* 68 (February 1962): 159-168.

————. "The Reference Library." *Analog Science Fact/Science Fiction* 69 (April 1962): 157-168.

————. "The Reference Library." *Analog Science Fact/Science Fiction* 69 (June 1962): 155-165.

————. "The Reference Library." *Analog Science Fact/Science Fiction* 69 (September 1962): 152-162.

————. "The Reference Library." *Analog Science Fact/Science Fiction* 70 (January 1963): 167-173.

————. "The Reference Library." *Analog Science Fact/Science Fiction* 72 (December 1963): 86-92.

————. "The Reference Library." *Analog Science Fact/Science Fiction* 73 (May 1964): 85-90.

————. "The Reference Library." *Analog Science Fiction/Science Fact* 74 (January 1965): 86-89.

————. "The Reference Library." *Analog Science Fiction/Science Fact* 76 (September 1965): 147-152.

————. "The Reference Library." *Analog Science Fiction/Science Fact* 76 (October 1965): 146-151.

————. "The Reference Library." *Analog Science Fiction/Science Fact* 77 (April 1966): 140-146.

————. "The Reference Library." *Analog Science Fiction/Science Fact* 77 (June 1966): 143-151.

————. "The Reference Library." *Analog Science Fiction/Science Fact* 78 (December 1966): 156-163.

————. "The Reference Library." *Analog Science Fiction/Science Fact* 79 (June 1967): 163-173.

————. "The Reference Library." *Analog Science Fiction/Science Fact* 79 (August 1967): 164-169.

————. "The Reference Library." *Analog Science Fiction/Science Fact* 81 (March 1968): 161-168.

————. "The Reference Library." *Analog Science Fiction/Science Fact* 82 (October 1968): 160-167.

————. "The Reference Library." *Analog Science Fiction/Science Fact* 82 (December 1968): 161-166.

————. "The Reference Library." *Analog Science Fiction/Science Fact* 83 (June 1969): 160-166.

————. "The Reference Library." *Analog Science Fiction/Science Fact* 84 (September 1969): 158-167.

————. "The Reference Library." *Analog Science Fiction/Science Fact* 85 (April 1970): 162-170.

————. "The Reference Library." *Analog Science Fiction/Science Fact* 85 (June 1970): 163-169.

————. "The Reference Library." *Analog Science Fiction/Science Fact* 86 (January 1971): 163-169.

————. "The Reference Library." *Analog Science Fiction/Science Fact* 87 (June 1971): 169-175.

————. "The Reference Library." *Analog Science Fiction/Science Fact* 87 (August 1971): 165-168.

————. "The Reference Library." *Analog Science Fiction/Science Fact* 88 (September 1971): 162-167.

————. "The Reference Library." *Analog Science Fiction/Science Fact* 88 (January 1972): 165-169.

————. "The Reference Library." *Analog Science Fiction/Science Fact* 88 (February 1972): 171-175.

————. "The Reference Library." *Analog Science Fiction/Science Fact* 89 (April 1972): 168-176.

————. "The Reference Library." *Analog Science Fiction/Science Fact* 89 (June 1972): 165-172.

————. "The Reference Library." *Analog Science Fiction/Science Fact* 90 (January 1973): 161-168.

————. "The Reference Library." *Analog Science Fiction/Science Fact* 91 (March 1973): 164-168.

————. "The Reference Library." *Analog Science Fiction/Science Fact* 91 (April 1973): 168-172.

————. "The Reference Library." *Analog Science Fiction/Science Fact* 91 (May 1973): 169-172.

————. "The Reference Library." *Analog Science Fiction/Science Fact* 91 (August 1973): 159-164.

————. "The Reference Library." *Analog Science Fiction/Science Fact* 92 (November 1973): 166-170.

————. "The Reference Library." *Analog Science Fiction/Science Fact* 92 (January 1974): 152-156.

————. "The Reference Library." *Analog Science Fiction/Science Fact* 93 (March 1974): 167-170.

————. "The Reference Library." *Analog Science Fiction/Science Fact* 93 (June 1974): 165-169.

————. "The Reference Library." *Analog Science Fiction/Science Fact* 93 (July 1974): 159-164.

————. "The Reference Library." *Analog Science Fiction/Science Fact* 94 (September 1974): 170-173.

Moskowitz, Sam. "How Science Fiction Got Its Name." In *Explorers of the Infinite: Shapers of Science Fiction*. Cleveland: World Publishing Company, 1963, 313-333. Originally published in *The Magazine of Fantasy and Science Fiction* in 1957.

————. "The Origins of Science Fiction Fandom: A Reconstruction." *Foundation: The Review of Science Fiction*, no. 48 (spring 1990): 5-25.

————. *Seekers of Tomorrow: Masters of Modern Science Fiction*. Cleveland: World Publishing Company, 1966.

Murdock, M. S. *Rebellion 2456. Martian Wars Trilogy #1*. A Buck Rogers Book. New York: TSR, 1989.

Nicholls, Peter. "Arthur C. Clarke." In *The Science Fiction Encyclopedia*, edited by Nicholls, 122-123.

————. "Hardcore SF." In *The Science Fiction Encyclopedia*, edited by Nicholls, 273.

————. "Hard SF." In *The Encyclopedia of Science Fiction*, edited by Clute and Nicholls, 542.

————. "Science Fiction: The Monsters and the Critics." In *Science Fiction at Large*, edited by Nicholls, 159-183.

————. "Soft SF." In *The Encyclopedia of Science Fiction*, edited by Clute and

Nicholls, 1131.

—————. "Soft SF." In *The Science Fiction Encyclopedia*, edited by Nicholls, 556.

—————, ed. *Science Fiction at Large: A Collection of Essays, by Various Hands, about the Interface between Science Fiction and Reality*. New York: Harper & Row, Publishers, 1976.

—————. *The Science Fiction Encyclopedia*. Garden City: Doubleday and Company, 1979.

Nicholls, Peter, and John Sladek. "Scientific Errors." In *The Science Fiction Encyclopedia*, edited by Nicholls, 532-533.

Niven, Larry. "Blowing Smoke." In *N-Space*, by Niven, 454-58.

—————. "Foreword." In *N-Space*, by Niven, 23-28.

—————. Interview with Jeffrey M. Elliot. In *Science Fiction Voices #2*, 9-19. Interview originally published in *Questar* in 1979.

—————. Introduction to an excerpt from *Ringworld*. In *N-Space*, by Niven, 122-124.

—————. *N-Space*. New York: TOR Books, 1990.

—————. *Ringworld*. New York: Ballantine Books, 1970.

Niven, Larry, with Jerry Pournelle. "Building The Mote in God's Eye." In *N-Space*,] by Niven, 339-360.

Parrinder, Patrick. *Science Fiction: Its Teaching and Criticism*. London: Methuen, 1980.

Philmus, Robert. "The Cybernetic Paradigms of Stanislaw Lem." In *Hard Science Fiction*, edited by Slusser and Rabkin, 177-213.

Pierce, John J. "The Literary Experience of Hard Science Fiction." *Science-Fiction Studies* 20 (July 1993): 176-183.

Rabkin, Eric S. *Arthur C. Clarke. Starmont Reader's Guide 1*. 1979. Mercer Island, Washington: Starmont House, 1980.

"The Reader Speaks" [Readers' letters and responses]. *Science Wonder Stories* 1 (June 1929): 92.

Rocklynne, Ross. "At the Center of Gravity." 1936. In *Exploring Other Worlds*. Edited by Sam Moskowitz. New York: Collier Books, 1963, 107-132. Originally published in *Astounding Stories* in 1936.

—————. "The Men and the Mirror." 1936. In *Before the Golden Age*. Edited by Isaac Asimov. Garden City: Doubleday and Company, 1974, 883-911. Story originally published in *Astounding Stories* in 1936.

Samuelson, David N. "Botching the Science in Science Fiction: Lambourne's *Close Encounters* and Zentz's *Jupiter's Ghost*." [Review article] *Science-Fiction Studies* 19 (March 1992): 100-104.

—————. "Modes of Extrapolation: The Formulas of Hard Science Fiction." *Science-Fiction Studies* 20 (July 1993): 191-232.

—————. Review of *Hard Science Fiction*, edited by Slusser and Rabkin. *Extrapolation* 27 (winter 1986): 357-360.

—————. "A Softening of the Hard-Sf Concept: Hartwell and Cramer's *The Ascent of Wonder*." [Review article] *Science-Fiction Studies* 21 (November 1994): 406-412.

The Science Fiction Writers of America. *Writing and Selling Science Fiction*. Cincinnati, Ohio: Writer's Digest, 1976.

Scortia, Thomas M. "Science Fiction as the Imaginary Experiment." In *Science Fiction: Today and Tomorrow*, edited by Bretnor, 135-147.

"The Secondary Universe." [no author given] *Locus*, Second Trial Issue (undated, 1968): [1].

Sheffield, Charles. *Between the Strokes of Night*. New York: Baen Books, 1985.

————. Letter. *Science Fiction Eye*, no. 10 (June 1992): 3-4.

Simak, Clifford D. *The Visitors*. 1979. New York: Del Rey\Ballantine Books, 1980.

Slusser, George. "The Ideal Worlds of Science Fiction." In *Hard Science Fiction*, edited by Slusser and Rabkin, 214-244.

————. "Reflections on Style in Science Fiction." In *Styles of Creation: Aesthetic Technique and the Creation of Fictional Worlds*. Edited by George Slusser and Eric S. Rabkin. Athens, Georgia: University of Georgia Press, 1992, 3-23.

————. *The Space Odysseys of Arthur C. Clarke*. San Bernardino, California: Borgo Press, 1978.

Slusser, George, and Eric S. Rabkin. "Introduction." In *Hard Science Fiction*, edited by Slusser and Rabkin, vii-xvi.

————, eds. *Hard Science Fiction*. Carbondale and Edwardsville, Illinois: Southern Illinois University Press, 1986.

Spinrad, Norman. "Dreams of Space." In *Science Fiction in the Real World*, by Spinrad, 122-135. Essay originally published in *Isaac Asimov's Science Fiction Magazine* in 1987.

————. "The Hard Stuff." In *Science Fiction in the Real World*, by Spinrad, 93-108. Essay originally published in *Isaac Asimov's Science Fiction Magazine* in 1988.

————. "Rubber Sciences." In *The Craft of Science Fiction*, edited by Bretnor, 54-9.

————. *Science Fiction in the Real World*. Carbondale, Illinois: Southern Illinois University Press, 1990.

Stableford, Brian. "Mars." In *The Science Fiction Encyclopedia*, edited by Nicholls, 381-383.

Sterling, Bruce. Interview with Takayuki Tatsumi. *Science Fiction Eye*, no. 1 (winter 1987): 27-42.

————. "Midnight on the Rue Jules Verne: Catscan." *Science Fiction Eye*, no. 1 (winter 1987): 62-64.

————. "Preface." In *Mirrorshades: The Cyberpunk Anthology*. Edited by Bruce Sterling. 1986. New York: Ace Books, 1988, ix-xvi.

Suvin, Darko. *Metamorphoses of Science Fiction: On the Poetics and History of a Literary Genre*. New Haven, Connecticut: Yale University Press, 1979.

Thomas, Lewis. *The Youngest Science: Notes of a Medicine-Watcher*. 1983. New York: Bantam Books, 1984.

von Noordung, Hermann. *The Problems of Space Flying*. 1929. Translated by Francis M. Currier. *Science Wonder Stories* 1 (July 1929): 170-180; (August 1929): 264-272; and (September 1929): 361-368. Originally published in Germany as *Das Problem der Befahrung des Weltraums*. Berlin: R. C. Schmidt & Co., 1929.

Walsh, J. M. *Vandals of the Void*. *Wonder Stories Quarterly* 2 (summer 1931): 458-

513.

Warrick, Patricia S. "Artificial Intelligence: Wild Imaginary Worlds, Wilder Realities." In *Hard Science Fiction*, edited by Slusser and Rabkin, 152-163.

Westfahl, Gary. "The Case against Space." *Monad: Essays on Science Fiction*, no. 4, forthcoming.

————. "'The Closely Reasoned Technological Story': The Critical History of Hard Science Fiction." *Science-Fiction Studies* 20 (July 1993): 157-175.

————. "'A Convenient Analog System': John W. Campbell, Jr.'s Theory of Science Fiction." *Foundation: The Review of Science Fiction*, no. 54 (spring 1992): 52-70.

————. "The Dance with Darkness: The Limits of Human Interest in Science Fiction." In *Evolutionary Aesthetics: Art in a Sociobiological Context*. Edited by Brett Cooke. Publisher and date of publication have not been determined.

————. "The Genre That Evolved: On Science Fiction as Children's Literature." *Foundation: The Review of Science Fiction*, no. 62 (winter 1994/1995): 70-75.

————. "Good Physics, Lousy Engineering: Arthur C. Clarke's *A Fall of Moondust*." *Monad: Essays on Science Fiction*, no. 3 (September 1993): 65-89.

————. "'An Idea of Significant Import': Hugo Gernsback's Theory of Science Fiction." *Foundation: The Review of Science Fiction*, no. 48 (spring 1990): 26-50.

————. *Islands in the Sky: The Space Station Theme in Science Fiction Literature*. Preface by Gregory Benford. San Bernardino, California: Borgo Press, 1995.

————. "On *The True History of Science Fiction*." *Foundation: The Review of Science Fiction*, no. 47 (winter/spring 1990): 5-27.

————. *The Other Side of the Sky: An Annotated Bibliography of Space Stations in Science Fiction, 1869-1993*. San Bernardino, California: Borgo Press, 1995.

Williams, Walter Jon. "Elegy for Angels and Dogs." *Isaac Asimov's Science Fiction Magazine* 14 (May 1990): 104-190.

Williamson, Jack. "Science Fiction, Teaching and Criticism." In *Science Fiction: Today and Tomorrow*, edited by Bretnor, 309-328.

————. "Short Stories and Novelettes." In *The Craft of Science Fiction*, edited by Bretnor, 195-213.

Wolfe, Gary K. "Reviews." *Locus* 32 (June 1994): 19, 21, 23, 62-63.

Wollheim, Donald A. *The Universe Makers: Science Fiction Today*. New York: Harper, 1971.

Wollheim, Donald A., and Terry Carr. Blurb to "Kyrie," by Poul Anderson. In *World's Best Science Fiction 1969*. Edited by Donald A. Wollheim and Terry Carr. New York: Ace Books, 1969, 33.

————. Blurb to "Sunjammer" ["The Wind from the Sun"], by Arthur C. Clarke. In *World's Best Science Fiction: 1966*. Edited by Donald A. Wollheim and Terry Carr. New York: Ace Books, 1966, 9.

Young, Louise B. "Mind and Order in the Universe." In *A Writer's Worlds: Explorations through Reading*. Edited by Trudy Smoke. New York: St. Martin's Press, 1990, 443-448. Originally published in 1986 in *The Unfinished Universe*, by Louise B. Young.

Zebrowski, George. *Macrolife*. New York: Harper & Row, Publishers, 1979.

Index

About the Author

GARY WESTFAHL teaches at the Learning Center of the University of California, Riverside. He has published numerous articles on science fiction and fantasy
in journals, magazines, critical anthologies, and reference books. He is also the
author of several forthcoming books on science fiction and fantasy and co-editor
of three forthcoming anthologies.

ISBN 0-313-29727-4

EAN

9 780313 297274

90000>

HARDCOVER BAR CODE